KLIPSPRINGER PRESS

# K

NEW YORK

http://klipspringerpress.com

Cover art by Jack Harrison Pinkerton Henson
Book design by archiefergusondesign.com

Edited by Jenna Bernstein

Published in 2018 by Klipspringer Press LLC. All rights reserved. No portion of this book may be reproduced, stored in a retrieval system, or transmitted in any form or by any means, mechanical, electronic, photocopying, recording, or otherwise, without written permission from the publisher.

ISBN: 978-0-9992319-2-0
eISBN: 978-09992319-3-7

Library of Congress Control Number: 2017949765

Printed in the United States
10 9 8 7 6 5 4 3 2 1

# Dear Jack

BARBARA BATES CONROY

JACKSON SCOTT CONROY

DEDICATED TO MY CHILDREN

Wilson Payton (Willie)

Harrison Steele (Harry)

Jackson Scott (Jackamo)

Henry Dickson (Hen)

Grace Harrison (Goose)


Written from my heart with love and devotion


Shanti Shanti Shanti

Peace Peace Peace

Special love and thank you to my friend and editor Jenna Bernstein. Jenna, a wise young lady, lovingly supported me through the months of editing, rewriting and discussing this manuscript. Holding me as I broke open.

Ho'opono opono

I'm sorry, please forgive me, thank you, I love you.

*September 2, 2016*

*Dear Jack,*

*It is September 2nd, your birthday. I am alone, on my sofa, on Martha's Vineyard, editing our book. This is my gift to you, Jack. I have not moved from this spot for the last nine hours, determined to complete the manuscript for you, for us and hopefully for others, on your twenty third birthday. At first, I thought that eight months of writing does not make for a very good book, but the fact is, I have been writing for twenty three years.*

*I am not attached to the outcome. It has been written. If I keep it tucked under my pillow to treasure, I'm fine with that. If our story can help someone gripped by addiction, so they can see the tragic outcome that lies ahead, or if the resources and my journey of healing can aid others suffering from grief, that would be my honor. I will continue on my journey of healing, seeking, and longing.*

*I know you are in good hands, loving hands. I only wish they were mine.*

*Love, Mom*

*July 31, 1993*

*Dearest baby,*

*Just two weeks to go before you arrive. It seems as though the past nine months I have been in another world. I have spent the last year, still to this very minute, grieving the loss of your sweet baby brother, Harry. Today, Daddy, Willie and I were at Lake View Cemetery watering the flowers and practicing stone throwing. We all miss our sweet baby, Harry, but I know in our hearts where he is, in heaven, where you have just come from.*

*We just bought a new home down at the beach in Bell Island. We are planning your nursery, not sure what colors, pink or blue?*

*Please forgive my tears, I don't know what feelings are in store. I thought that a new life would fill the bleeding hole in my heart, but I am learning now that your life is unique and will never fill the hole but will offer our little family new joy, different joy. Now I feel loving is so hard, I am also so frightened of the possibilities, the dangers of life.*

*"To love is to risk losing*
*To lose is to risk finding something new*
*The cycle of the heart*
*Birth*
*Death*
*Rebirth*

*Therefore, before my heart turns to stone, I will re-enter the cycle and make up my mind again to risk loving."*
—Safe Passage, *Molly Fumia*

*With love,*
*Mommy xo*

**APRIL 1, 2015.** A day like any other. Standing at my kitchen counter, making my coffee, breakfast is underway for Grace. "Five more minutes," she said. She always wants five more minutes to sleep.

The phone rings. I hate the phone, it scares me.

I am always afraid when the phone rings, I have a lot of kids, Jack always in trouble. Most calls are bad news, I hate the phone.

It's Kevin, "Jack is dead."

Oh my God, oh my God no no no no. That is all I could say, I could hear that noise, that guttural wailing. No no no no. Oh my God. I ran to Grace she screamed the same. Oh my God no no no no. I don't know what else happened. I have no idea, I just circled around my kitchen counter saying the same thing, Oh my God, no no no no NO. Oh My God!

*September 2, 1993*
*11 pounds 3/4 ounces*
*22 1/4 inches*

*What a big baby!*

*The feelings were so overwhelming, feelings of love, apprehension, praise, fear, everything all rolled up in tears.*

*Everyone has been in to see you, they have all been waiting for you to come. It is time to go home, Daddy and Willie are coming to pick us up. We still haven't completely decided your name. We know it is baby Jack, but trying to figure out the rest. I'll write them here and Daddy can choose one when he arrives.*

*Jackson Scott Conroy   xoxoxoxo*
*Jackson Steele Conroy*
*Jack Harrison Conroy*
*John Harrison Conroy*

*September 4, 1993*

*Dearest Baby Jack,*

*You are so fresh from Heaven. Thanks be to God! You are a beautiful baby, you are so like Harry, it brings Mommy and Daddy such joy. Willie adores you, lots of cuddles and snuggles. Delivery was longer than I thought. Started at home at about 10 PM. Daddy suggested I relax and go to the hospital in the morning. We ended up in the hospital at 1:00 in the morning. I had an epidural at about 3:00 and you were born at 7:20 AM.*

*October 5, 1993*

*Dearest Baby Jack,*

*Wow, time really flies. You are now five weeks old. Since you were born so much has happened. Our new pastor and the ladies from church had a shower for you. It was so beautiful. I am so glad you were there. Beautiful lunch and gifts all for the celebration of your life. Always remember your Noah's Ark and how special it is.*

*We remembered the anniversary of the death of your sweet baby brother, Harry. We adore him and miss him so much. I thought you would replace or fill the hole, heal the wound, but it is still there. And I just love you for you, I wish I had you both.*

*Wee Robert was born, everyone is doing great. I've been spending so much time writing thank you notes for ALL of the beautiful gifts for you. I'll try to keep them in good shape. Oh, how could I forget. We sold our home in town and moved into a rental across from Auntie Leslie. We are renovating our new home down at the beach.*

*Willie adores you! Lots of kisses and hugs. Lots of smiles and sweet noises from you. They touch our hearts more than you could ever know. Granny has been such a wonderful help to us and to Auntie Cathy. We are very blessed to have such wonderful family and friends.*

*I love you, God bless you sweet baby.*

*Love, mommy xo*

*May 30, 1997*

*Jackamo I love you.*

    *You are always a sweet boy. You take such good care of your brother, Henry. You are always helping Mommy and now you are loving your new baby sister. Baby Grace our special gift from God. You are always complementing your new baby sister on her "beautiful dress" or "beautiful hair." Sweet boy. What are the chances of Willie and Grace to be born on the same day!*

    *You had a great year at school. You have lots of friends. School's out now for summer and you will be starting camp soon at Roton Point. You are very busy riding your bike and you want to start riding Pumpkin again.*

    *I love you Jack, to the moon and back*

    *love mommy  xo*

*Jack's birthday breakfast*

# JACKAMO

Our little boy stole everyone's heart from the beginning. He was a happy little/big boy. He adored his big brother, Willie. He adored us. He was love. That's what happens when you come from the Source, you are pure love.

One day when Jack was still very small we went out to the movies as a family, Kevin, Willie, Jack and me. The animated film *Thumbelina* was playing in our local theater. Willie loved all the animated movies, so we went. One of the characters was a little bird. He was French. His name was Jacquimo. He helped Thumbelina, rescuing her from danger and serving her from then on. The name caught on, and it stuck. Perfect for our helpful boy. We began calling him Jackamo.

Jackamo was the snuggliest, sweetest love from the start. Always wanted to be where the action was and such a big helper. He loved to help out with everything he could, gardening, cooking, errands. He would help neighbors clean up, babysit, and he even chased a snake out of our friend Suellan's cottage. When my cement basement flooded only a couple of feet, and we had to find the water pump to make sure it was still pumping water out of the basement, Jack put on his swimming goggles and kicked through the flood to find the equipment. He was little, maybe five.

Jack was always first up on Easter morning and first to scope outside to see if he could see the candy and toy-filled baskets. He would determine which was whose and he would fetch them for everyone. Well, most times, but always for himself and for his little sister, Grace. I was watching a video (I have tons of home movies, thank God!) of Jack running for the baskets. I said, "Jack, are you going to go back out and get the other baskets?" In his little cotton pajamas he was holding his foot with both hands, and he said, "Yes," in his sweet little boy raspy morning voice. "I'm just warming up my feet." Then off he went. Easter is in spring, but it was cold that year. Didn't stop

Jackamo, though.

He was always like that, jumping into action. When he was older, Jack would catch fish, scale them and have them filleted for dinner. He was excellent on the grill. Every time I clean the grill I think of him. He would use two hands and press firmly for the best results. I don't do nearly the job that he did.

Jack was a big help at birthday parties, too. At Grace's birthday he asked if he could help. Now that I think of it, he was supposed to be in school, as Grace's nursery school had already finished. Anyway, he was home and he helped run the party games. Lining up all the little girls by the game of corn hole to throw little sacks into a clown's mouth that I painted on a board, or throwing rings around tootsie pops to win one.

One year, Grace had a Hawaiian themed party. Grace and her friends wore colored grass skirts and bathing suit tops, so adorable. I happened to have an employee who lived in Hawaii, and she taught them hula dancing. Floral wreaths crowned the girls' hair. Jack's too! He was there helping and learning the dance.

I always make such a big deal of birthdays. My birthdays growing up were special. My mom would have a little pile of gifts ready for me when I woke up, there was always a bowl of M&M's, too. My birthday is in August; no one was ever around in the summer. The few friends that were still in town would come over for a birthday barbecue. My childhood friend, Lisa, still sends me a text every year on my birthday asking what's on the grill. I can remember opening the back door and hearing the locusts and feeling the warm breeze blowing in. Life was simple then.

When I got to be the one throwing the party for my kids, I always wanted them to be special, too. All the celebrations in my house were BIG, including all the holidays. This highlights my type A personality.

Maybe it was out of guilt? Maybe. I worked hard in New York City, at a high-paying job. I traveled a lot. I had help, nannies and cleaners. My kids were well cared for, and their dad worked in our hometown. By my book, we had a perfect life.

Nothing was too good for my kids. On their birthdays, I made heart waffles, balloons and party blowers. We would wake up and take pictures first thing, always in the morning, so our birthday photos were with morning hairdos and morning eyes. Then we opened the gifts. I loved going all out, over-the-top for their parties. We had farm birthdays, with livestock and pony rides, big bounce houses on the front lawn, bubble birthdays, surprise parties. Jack's birthday usually happened either on the beach or the boat. Even when he was a teenager, I would ask if he wanted a fishing birthday. One year the party favor for Jack's fishing birthday at East Beach was a goldfish in a small glass fish bowl. I thought it would be cute. Bad idea, as it was too warm out and they started floating to the top. I quickly got the ones still swimming back home to safety.

Fourth of July was big a deal, too. Every year the festivities started Friday night with the Bell Island Lobster Bake. That is where I first laid eyes on Kevin. In my 20s, I rented a house on Bell Island and went to the lobster bake. He was standing in front of me in line—nice butt! Fast forward many years and we were still on Bell Island, gathering for the feast with all our neighbors, family and friends.

Saturday morning of the Fourth of July weekend began with the parade. This was important. We had a small trailer on which year after year we would build our family float. Most original, most patriotic, funniest, most creative, we won every year. I put some serious elbow grease into those floats. We had The Olympic's Float, with speedos and goggles for our little Olympians, The Rock Band Float, complete with fake piercings, and red and blue hair for all, The Army Float, where everyone wore camouflage, but the real winner was the Mystery Machine Float, with all the Scooby Doo characters inside. All the cousins would show up to play their part, and to play in the Fourth of July games.

From age one to eighteen, Jack participated with everyone in the games, toddling on the basketball court carrying his bucket for the lollypop scramble, to later the three legged and wheel barrow races. But Jack championed the potato sack race. At our last game day, all the big boys sat up on the beach wall, too cool to participate. Then it came time. The announcer said, "Grab Your Sacks!" I looked at Jack on the wall and said, "Come on Jack, this is your race."

"You really want me to do this, Mom? I'm going to win," he said. "Mm-Hmm."

Ready. Set. Go! Jack's sack came up to the middle of his thighs. Holding the sack with his right hand, his left arm swinging to get the momentum, he was off. Bounce, bounce, bounce, turn around, bounce, bounce, bounce, he was back at the finish line! Won again. Six bounces, that's nuts! It was a small playground, but still.

Family vacations were another highlight. St. John's was one of our family favorites. I have so many videos. I watch them all the time. One video was on a snorkeling trip organized by our hotel. As the interviewer, I asked Will where we were. He replied, "On a snorkeling cruise." Continuing my interview, I found Jack and his rosy cheeks. I said, "Jack, what's your name?" "You just said it," he said. "Where are we Jack?" "Whistling Key," he said. He was eight. He always had a solid sense of his surroundings, he was always listening, but, not always to me. I would say, "Jack how is your behavior?" "Good," he would always say. "Bad" is what I would say.

All of these memories bring a smile to my face. That was his true essence. He was a good boy.

One time we were all on Lucy Vincent Beach on Martha's Vineyard. It was my daughter Grace and her friend Carly, her mother and my dear friend, Judy, me, and Jack. Jack was sixteen, Grace and Carly were twelve years old. Somehow, Jack managed to fill his backpack with ten beers or so, and still insisted he wasn't drinking. Is that the craziest thing? Carly and Grace were in the ocean bobbing up and down. Jack was asleep while Judy and I chatted. I saw Carly's arms waving back and forth. I couldn't hear with the tumbling waves, but they were screaming.

Grace and Carly were caught in a rip tide. I said, "Judy, oh my God, the girls are stuck." Jack, lying next to us sunbathing on a towel, opened his bloodshot eyes and ran down the beach and through the waves. He was so strong, plunging in and swimming out to the girls. He grabbed them both and swam them to shore. He could do anything, and that was more than helping. When they reached the shore, a beer can was left behind in the waves.

Sometimes Jack would help our neighbor Georgie, at home in Rowayton, with her kids and her cleaning. Georgie's garage was full of the latest toys and bikes and jumpy things. Jack was always a big help. She was on Team Jack.

She called me recently to tell me she had a vivid dream about Jack. She said, in the dream, he was helping her move. He had to move her turtles because they were "very temperamental." Hmmm. "Do you have turtles?" I asked. She did; she had four. I didn't know that. I imagined the little plastic dish with the palm tree in the center, like the one I kept my turtles in when I was little.

*Jack helping Grace with Easter baskets.*

*December 5, 2015*

*Dear Jack,*

    *I am here on Martha's Vineyard, very peaceful and beautiful. I wish you had spent more time here. I guess you were in rehab. You missed so much with us during those years. Now we can never get it back. I spoke with Georgie for an hour yesterday while driving up here. She had a dream about you. You were helping her move and helped with her turtles. She went on about how you always helped her move things around and helped with the kids. (They thought it was so cool that they had Jack as a baby sitter.)*

    *Days later I had a phone call with a psychic medium in Colorado and you came through. You always show up, you are trying to help me. Even now, you are helping. She said, "I am just going to say this because Jack has said it four times, and I don't know what it means." "Turtles," she said. "Does that mean anything to you?" "Yes, it does."*

    *Yes, it was him.*

    *It was so sweet Georgie called to tell me about it. We talked so long about her situation with her husband. Maybe you sent her to me for a new perspective. I hope I helped her because bad shit happens anyway, why cause it yourself. She needs peace, not craziness. Her kids need stability and certainty. Right Jack? Is that what messed you up? Was it me and Dad? It was messed up, I wish it never happened, I wish none of this happened and we would be getting ready for Christmas with all of us and all the family together.*

*Art Journal page, Island Life*

*Summer fishing for striped bass, Dad*
*and Jack, Martha's Vineyard*

# ROMANS 8

I never liked to sit up front at church, but that day I was in the front pew. I had been in this space so many times. The walls were a light pink, I always liked that, the arched windows had white trim, and let in beautiful bright light. Willie was baptized here. Harry was never baptized, we didn't have time. The cross was on the wall behind where the choir sat, but there was no choir. This space was so familiar, but that day I was in the front, I'm never in the front.

Behind me were hundreds of friends, co workers, I had no idea who else. I don't remember this time so well. So much grief, so much pain. My family surrounded me. I felt dazed and dizzy. Kevin, my husband, sat next to me. My mom and dad were there, Granny and Papa of course, and Kevin's mom and dad too, Nonie and Pops. All of our siblings. I have three, Leslie is two years older then me, Cathy a few years younger, and then Robert, who I affectionately call Jol. (Short for Jolly.) Kevin's siblings, so many, Regina, Bill, John, Brian, or Ryan, or Grayson, he kept changing his name, then Chris. A large family, we were all in the front. I hate the front.

> *"For I am convinced that neither death nor life, neither angels nor demons, neither the present nor the future, nor any powers, neither height nor depth, nor anything else in all creation, will be able to separate us from the love of God or me."* Romans 8:38

I stared at her eyes, blue and teary. She looked back at me. It was as though God spoke the words from the Romans verse directly to me at Harry's memorial service. Not to everyone in the congregation, but to me. It was the new associate pastor that was sharing this message to my grief struck family and the rest of the congregation.

It was September 25, 1992. She came to the hospital emergency room the night it happened. When I saw her come in, I knew it was terrible news. She seemed like an angel. I could see heaven through her eyes. Her skin was so pale, like porcelain. I was sure her skin never saw the sun, which I worshipped. Romans 8 was how it was with me and Jack, but I said it differently, no one can separate him from the love of God, or me. Call it blasphemy, whatever. Nothing Jack did or said could separate him from me. It became a theme in my love letters to Jack as he got older. "I love you no matter what." Like a mantra. Nothing could shake that. Over the years I was pretty rattled.

Jack's high school graduation was a close call for sure. Weeks and days leading up to graduation day, it was uncertain whether or not Jack would have enough credits to walk. I thought he could make up the credits in summer school. Damn, I wanted him to graduate so much. If you were cleared to walk you received your cap and gown. Days to go and no cap and gown. Jack and I had been on a rocky road. He struggled with partying and keeping up with his academics. It didn't matter that he was a star athlete, and that he had already been accepted to a college where he would play on the lacrosse team. If he didn't have the credits, he couldn't graduate. I didn't know if the rough patch was over. He seemed to finally be on track, but I was still afraid, and he was still running a few credits short. Then, a science teacher came through and had Jack clean up the classroom for .25 credits.

He did it!!! Jack was graduating high school! I was so happy and excited, I think he was too. I planned a big graduation party for him, the invitation read, "It Takes a Village." All of Jack's friends came and my family and friends too. It was a milestone worth celebrating, and he did it! I was so proud to see him walk in his royal blue gown. I bought a Diane von Furstenberg dress, white with a royal blue pattern, to match. I added some great white strappy shoes to complete the look. I bought cigars, catered lots of food and drinks. I can't remember all that we had to eat, but I know we had sushi. We loved sushi, Jack and me. Getting Jack through high school had been no easy feat, but now he had done it, with lots of help from family and friends. It truly took a village, everyone there was a significant part of Jack's life. I put together a slideshow collection of my favorite photos of Jack and displayed it on a big computer screen to show him and the guests. Pictures of him from his early days, pictures of him with friends and family, pictures from the Vineyard. I made digital photo books along with the home movie compilation for each of my kids when they graduated. I loved doing it, reliving all those sweet moments in our lives. The first picture in Jack's book was him with the Romans quote.

*"For I am convinced that neither death nor life, neither angels nor demons, neither the present nor the future, nor any powers, neither height nor depth, nor anything else in all creation, will be able to separate us from the love of God or me."*

A few years later, when the entire congregation returned to our home following Jack's memorial service, his slideshow was already prepared and the movie was playing, along with his favorite music, rap, full of cursing and drug references. Not necessarily appropriate for a memorial service, but who cares?

Back in the church again. The Saturday before Easter, April 2015. The Sanctuary was already filled with Easter lillies. It was supposed to be a celebration, Easter. But it was a different kind of celebration that year, for Jack. Another milestone. This celebration was of his life. I asked Kevin and my children if they would like to speak at the memorial, they all said yes.

Kevin spoke first. We didn't think he was going to make it, either that or once he got up there he would keep talking, which would have been worse. He worked on his talk with his brother, John, all day. He greeted and welcomed the congregation, then he spoke about the internal rattling within Jack, it was like a poem.

Grace knew right away what she wanted to say. Imagine these kids having to stand up and speak about their brother, it was heartbreaking. Grace said Jack was like a bad puppy, you could hit him on the nose with a newspaper, and then forgive him right away. She was so beautiful and confident, Jack loved her. As she said, he was her best friend.

Henry, so tall and handsome, a true gentleman, spoke of how Jack protected him from the minute he was born. Jack only one year old, climbed into the little plastic bassinet in the hospital while newborn Henry slept in the pink and blue striped blanket. Henry also spoke about my "traps" (trapezius muscles), and how big they were because I carried so much of the burden. My "traps" Will says, made me look like a football player. Henry did a beautiful job, he made everyone laugh. He told a story of Jack applying for a job cleaning the outside of buildings, rappelling down the side. They said five years experience needed. Jack signed up, with no experience, and no surprise, he got the job.

Will, my oldest, spoke after me because he was going to sing. He stood in the oh so familiar church, the same light pink walls, sun shining in. Kevin said to me, while Will began to speak, "He doesn't have anything prepared." What would make Kevin think Will would prepare something? It was just not his thing. He freestyles, he's a performer. Will said, "Being a member of the church, doesn't make you a good Christian, wearing a suit doesn't mean you're not a hippie," (Will's hair was quite long, he usually sports a man bun.) "and having the same last name doesn't make you a good brother." So heavy, the grief and guilt.

He was so handsome, in his suit, he loves his suit. He sang a beautiful song, "Return to Sender," by Ricky Skaggs, (not Elvis). Will has a beautiful voice, and is an amazing guitarist, artist. Harry gave him a guitar as a present when he came home from the hospital. He has never put it down. All so familiar. All my kids were in the choir, in the bands, confirmation.

My nephew Andrew sang a beautiful original song, "Lying to Myself." I always thought he wrote it about Kevin, but maybe it was about Jack. My other nephews Kenny, Christian and Cameron played beautiful music as the congregation entered the sanctuary. Kenny led the group in "Amazing Grace." Afterward he said, "What was I thinking, singing "Amazing Grace" by myself." So talented my family.

Emily, Jack's girlfriend spoke too. She read from a letter Jack had written to her. He wrote that they would be "surfer chic and bra" together. She described how Jack had to pick his nose with his pinky, his other fingers were too big.

It seemed like mine was already in my head, it just poured out on to the

*Jack loving his new baby, Henry,*
*February 12, 1995*

*Will's and Jack's last time together,*
*Pacific Ocean.*

*Grace and Jack, Christmas 2014,*
*Carlsbad, CA*

paper. I stepped up to the podium, all those people in the balcony and also outside and downstairs. A large poster of me reaching up and kissing Jack's cheek hung from the alter where I spoke. It was taken on his graduation day. He was wearing his blue gown, I was wearing my matching blue dress. I was so proud.

I wanted to speak slowly, and with love and intention dedicate my words to Jack. I chose the images that were displayed throughout the church, the photo on the program. I chose the music we would sing and the food we would eat after returning to my home. I don't know who did that for Harry, it wasn't me, it happened without me. Not this time...

I began my speech.

"For I am convinced that neither death nor life, neither angels nor demons, neither the present nor the future, nor any powers, neither height nor depth, nor anything else in all creation, will be able to separate us from the love of God or me." Romans 8:38

*Me and Jack, graduation day. June 2011*

*Family Christmas Dinner*

*December, 22, 1993*

*Dearest Baby Jack,*

*Christmas is almost here! So much hustle and bustle. We are still in the rental house. Daddy is out Christmas shopping. I just put Willie in his bed and you are in your basket by my bed. You are very snuggly and cozy after you and Willie took a bath.*

*Last week at your 3 1/2 months visit you weighed in at 19 pounds, 28 1/2 inches long. Dr. T. said that you are the size of a nine month old!!*

*Willie has written your Christmas list to Santa.*

*Happy Birthday Jesus!*
*Merry Christmas*

*You have started applesauce and cereal. YUM YUM!*

*You are the happiest snuggly little boy. We love you so much. Sorry when Willie is so rough.*

*Merry Christmas*

*Amen xo*

*We Without You by Lisa Swerling and Ralph Lazar*

# CHRISTMAS HERE AND THERE

Christmas, the most special day of the year. I have them all recorded. Tons of videos and photos. So many videos that are sideways, the camera left on the table still recording, but some good ones too. One has been so much in the forefront of my mind. Jack was one and a half. Always the first up due to all of the excitement the night before. Santa's coming, cookies and milk are out, carrots in place for the reindeer. How could anyone even sleep? Kevin and I would be up in the middle of the night wrapping and setting everything up, piles of toys for Jack and Willie and well, Henry was just a baby so he just needed boxes. Looking at the piles with the tree lit in the background, it was magical. Christmas morning I would sit quietly before all the chaos was to begin, drinking a hot cup of coffee, staring at the tree. I would go a little cross eyed, so that I could focus on the lights only, everything else dropping back in the distance.

Jack was such a little monkey, able to climb out of his crib. His pajamas that morning in the video were a little red tartan flannel set, his hair was white blond and straight, so funny that he ended up with his luxurious wavy brown hair. His eyebrows were so blond we couldn't even see them. He was the first one up, it was time to wake up Willie. I followed behind him up the stairs with the video camera. We went up to Willie's room and he climbed in his bed. Willie was still sound asleep under his purple Aladdin flannel sheets. "Willie, Willie (with that sweet little W sound ) it's Christmas and I got Spot." Jack found his pile right away because on top was the stuffed yellow dog, Spot, from a story book he loved. He tucked spot under his arm and that is where he stayed for years, "My Spot."

When it was time to say goodbye, I got a Spot to tuck under Jack's arm, right where he belonged. It was a larger puppy than the original Spot, but Jack was a big boy now.

Christmas, the most special day. Following gifts came yummy breakfast, fried eggs, Scottish bacon and toast. It was clean up time, 'cause all the cousins would be over in no time at all. Then it happened all over again! Gifts, wrapping everywhere, music and traditional dinner. Roast beef, had to be rare! I ended up with four or five meat thermometers, for fear that the meat would be over cooked. If that happened my father would be in a bad mood the entire dinner. (Surprising for a Scottish man. The only meat I ever had growing up on our trips "hame" to Scotland, was like eating an old boot. Meat seemed to cook for hours.) Yorkshire pudding, roast potatoes and brussels sprouts. We all popped our poppers and wore the colorful paper crowns on our heads, told the jokes that were inside, sang songs and lit the plumb pudding on fire. First the pudding was doused in brandy. Usually someone caught on fire, most often Uncle Rob, my brother.

Last December was the first in twenty years that we did not have that traditional Christmas. After a rough few years in and out of rehab and school, Jack was finally stable, in a program and seemed to be on a healthy track. I said if Jack was doing well we would come to him in California that year. We agreed that coming back home had too many triggers and it would be safer for him to stay in Cali. He was doing well, so Grace, Henry and I flew to San Diego from Connecticut. Will flew in from Nashville. We all met at Jack's new apartment and met his new girlfriend, Emily.

Pacific Beach was hip, and Jack lived a block from the water. Wow! I felt so happy for him. He and Emily were living together, which of course was against the rules in his AA program. He just wanted to get on with his life, and not sit in a room of drug addicts and drunks and repeat the mantra, "I am a drug addict." Pacific Beach was a young crowd, everyone was out exercising and surfing and eating healthy. Avocados from California, quinoa, and acai bowls, were his favorites. He loved surfing. Being so close to the water, he would be out in the surf by seven in the morning. Kevin bought him a great surf board and wet suit. The water looked like it was filled with seals, all the little black spots were surfers.

This was a good life for Jack. He and Emily were dating for about seven months. She was a good influence. She came from a nice Christian family, she loved to eat healthy food and loved the beach too. She did not do drugs, nor drink much. She was attending fashion school in Los Angeles. I liked her, and still do.

We rented a great house in Carlsbad and had a somewhat tense Christmas breakfast. Poppers were included and crowns were worn by all. Words had not been shared between Jack and Will, which made it feel like a time bomb was about to go off, but we managed through it anyway. I gave Jack a little book, *We Without You*, by Lisa Swerling and Ralph Lazar. I chose this as his gift because lately he seemed so disconnected from us, after all that went on, the drugs, lying, stealing.

We were all wounded, but we were there. I ask myself now, why would I get such a book? A little cartoon book, that page after page would illustrate and say, "We without you is like crafts without glue, bolt without screw, old Mc Donald without moo. We without you? It just wouldn't be right! Like apple without bite, boo without fright, cloud without white, day without sunlight. We without you? There's no way! Like waiter without tray, elephant without gray, disco with out DJ. We without you, oh me oh my! Like bath without dry, shoelace without tie, needle without eye. We without you? Like rainbow without hue."

I gave him the little book on Christmas morning. There were only three characters in all the drawings, so I added in two more, now there were five, me, Jack, Will, Henry and Grace. We signed it for him, we wanted Jack back in our lives. Family vacations maybe? Visiting Will in Nashville? Just normal family things. Conversations about something other than drugs, or legal problems. Not having my heart stop when his name came across my phone.

This was going to be a great year, 2015. Jack was happy and healthy. Emily was now in his life, a wonderful young lady and influence. Jack lived in California loving everything, the water and sand, surfing, organic food. He needed to get a job... but other than that, things were looking good!

Why would I get that book? We are without you.

Christmas, the most special day of the year. This year Christmas didn't come. No Christmas dinner, no piles of gifts, no songs or flaming plumb pudding. I left and went on a trip alone. Me Without You...

*Christmas in Cali*

*December 26, 2015*

*Dear Jack,*

*All I wanted for Christmas was you and I didn't get it. I traveled all the way to TCI (Turks and Caicos Island). I was alone and thinking of you. Seeing the pool and remembering you, Grace and the Sullivans splashing around when we spent spring break all together. And even in the airport, the seats you and Grace sat in across from me. You were wearing the backyard funk T shirt with the green sleeves. I have the picture.*

*I didn't have Christmas morning, I couldn't do it. We did have a nice dinner at Uncle Rob's when I got back. I heard from Emily. She sent me a photo of you both at Christmas last year that I hadn't seen. You look happy. I've been working on another journal, making my celebration list and continuing to talk to my inner child, helping to support her sadness. I wish I had these tools to use to help you. I was so concerned with my fear and pain instead of helping you with yours. I understand now that addiction is just hiding pain.*

*Merry Christmas Jackamo, I love you*

*Jack and Carlyn in ustrasana in my living room yoga studio, February, 2015*

# WHO AM I, WHERE AM I, WHAT AM I DOING?

I can't count the times I have been instructed to be present. I am for a second, then the thoughts start flooding in, self-talk (mostly negative), the things to do for the day, month, year, and everything from the past, which is now just a memory, in my mind. All of the future, which hasn't happened yet, in my mind. The only thing that is real is the present. (It is already the past, happens that fast.) Everything else is mostly in the mind. All of those dreams, what-ifs, possible futures or pasts... It isn't real, it is imagination.

My Martha's Vineyard yoga teacher, or goddess rather, is named Sherry. I stumbled upon her class many years ago. She is a beautiful woman inside and out, and has taught me so many things about the ancient tradition and teachings of yoga. Whether in the studio or walking on the beach, we dive deep. A classic "Sherryism" is to say to yourself or out loud, "Who am I, where am I, what am I doing?" It grounds you, and strips away all of the unreal. Clean slate.

I am Barbara, I am on Martha's Vineyard, on my sofa. I am typing pages for Jack and my book. That's it! All the rest is my imagination.

It is an enormous effort to be present. Tuned in. And it definitely takes practice, being aware of those fleeting thoughts. They never stop. I just notice them and try not to let them take residence in my mind. They can float on by. They can't be ignored, I don't think. I have not figured that out. Just notice, and try to come back to center, to me. Getting rid of the clouds, the things in my way, what Sherry calls "interference," helps with clarity. The practice of yoga helps me with this. Its many teachings and philosophies have been woven into the fabric of my life. It's become a new way of understanding the world, and myself.

My yoga journey began with trying to get fit. How you get to yoga doesn't matter, Sherry says, yoga does you without you even realizing it. It becomes you.

I started with sweaty Bikram Yoga. Hot, dark room, same poses done twice. Eh. It was good in February in the Northeast, cold, dark, damp. Hot was good. But on a sunny day, it didn't work for me. Some people love it. Knowing exactly what comes next, the same poses every time. Personally I like surprise. I like variety in the different postures so I can sincerely focus on the instruction and my internal landscape and nothing else. I am Barbara, on my mat, in tree pose. That's it.

I decided to sign up for a yoga teacher training with my local teacher Bernadette in Connecticut during the fall of 2012. I had the time and wanted to deepen my practice. Two-hundred hour teacher training underway. Day one we wrote letters to ourselves stating our intention. I wrote:

*Dear Barbara,*

*I have no intention of teaching yoga, I want to learn more about the practice and philosophy as a self discovery.*

When we completed our training, I couldn't contain myself and all that I had learned. I returned home and removed all the furniture in my living room and opened my own studio named "My Yoga." I had business cards made, created a Facebook page, and hung posters in the local shops in town.

I had to share what I had learned. It is not something to keep to yourself. I taught eight classes a week including my favorite teen yoga class. I carefully planned the sequences for my classes at first (after a while, the sequences happened organically, not with all the planning), and compiled a great playlist to match. I loved it. My teen yogis, ages twelve and thirteen, were my most dedicated. I taught them for two years and they never missed a class. I changed up their playlist to include some of their favorite pop singers. We would all sing, a great way to practice pranayama, or breath work. We had some laughs for sure. Maisy, Mia, Chloe, Maggie and Angie, my loves. We are still on a group chat together. I incorporated dancing, spinning and shaking into our practice. I learned these practices in Sherry's classes. These ancient practices are different forms of yoga.

Shakti dance integrates free flowing movement into the yoga practice. Historically, it's a way to bring people together, connecting with ourselves and to each other. The practice returns us to human interaction, connection. In Sanskrit, the ancient, sacred language of Hinduism, the word "Shakti" describes the force that animates life. The dance takes the practitioner out of the thinking mind and into the body. Cranking the music up, the dance would turn into a train that went through my kitchen and out the front door, a spin around the yard and back to the mat.

Sufi spinning is a physically active meditation. The original aim was to reach toward the source of perfection, God. The girls liked to spin until they were dizzy. Innocence, "inner sense," Sherry would say. We would form a circle and one of the girls jumped into the middle. Next, the person in the middle extends the right arm with the hand facing towards the face and focuses on the palm of their hand. The practitioner in the middle begins to spin to the right. While the world is spinning, the practitioner focuses solely on the hand. After a minute or so, the spinner stops abruptly and stares at something that is not moving until they feel stable, like the world is no longer spinning. All the others around the circle are there for safety, to catch the person in the middle in case they fall. All there for each other. Once it was over, the girls laughed and laughed.

Shaking yoga is about self healing. Healing the body and clearing the mind, the thoughts we cling to. We would shake the hands, the arms the feet, the legs, and try our best to shake the torso, jumping up and down. Shaking out everything we held on to. Generating high energy and inner heat to do so. They didn't know all of this, we were all having fun, but yoga gets to you without you even realizing it.

My yogi girls were among the first to come to my house when they found out Jack died. They made beautiful posters and included the teachings we incorporated into the practice on paper. Beautiful heartfelt letters of love and support. I think they kind of had a crush on Jack. He would come to the living room when they were there and they would giggle. He took my class once, with just one other student, Carlyn, Maisy's mom. I was amazed that a man of his size was so agile. So strong but flexible. He knew all the poses; I guess they practiced at the different rehabs. I have a photo of him in ustrasana, camel pose. Heart open, on knees reaching back and holding his heels. It made me very happy to share yoga with him. He was light on his feet, and always well connected to his body with his natural athletic abilities.

I am Jack, in camel pose, in my living room.

I wish I was able to teach him to return to himself, to just be, without all the chaos that whirled around him.

My real understanding of the science of yoga came from Sherry, more than from my original training. I jumped into her mid-spring teacher's immersion on Martha's Vineyard, and it changed the trajectory of my life.

Sherry's classes were different than what I was accustomed to, but I liked them, and I got hooked. You never know what to expect with Sherry's classes. I had been practicing a very similar routine, class after class for years. Sit at the front of the mat, repeat the same mantra three times, followed by Om, it became routine. But Sherry's class always felt charged, with energy, physicality, spirituality and power. I was hooked, on the practice, the teachings, the music, and ultimately the friendship. Oh yeah, and the yoga poses.

I spent the year following my yoga teacher training seeking out new modalities for healing, on and off the island. I began to study different traditions as well. I commuted to New York to study medicinal oils at the Open School and became certified. I was intrigued by all the essences, which are so complicated. It was like a "farm-acy." All the flowers and herbs from all over the world, creating healing for ourselves. Peppermint behind the ear for cooling, flower essences on the pillow for sweet dreams, essences for sleep, anxiety, digestive problems, you name it. I bought in, purchased my supplies, and used them in my yoga classes.

I took level one and two reiki training, also on Martha's Vineyard. Healing hands. While practicing with my partner, I put her to sleep. Deep relaxation. The practice of reiki is designed to channel energy from the practitioner to the client, to activate natural healing and emotional well being. I still have one more level to go to become certified.

Three summers ago, Sherry asked if I would assist her teacher training in the summer on the island. I responded, "Yes" right away. This would be a perfect summer job. I would expand my teaching knowledge, and I would be on Martha's Vineyard!

I had no idea what I was getting into. I thought I would be getting her coffee. She knew better. She knew I needed to do the training. And that is exactly what happened. I met my good friend Meghan there as we were both assisting Sherry, and we went through the entire training together. Thank God! Meghan is a resident here on Martha's Vineyard and has a love for "up island" life like me. The remote town of Aquinnah is her love, her sacred space. It is slow-paced, rural life, as opposed to the busy commercial towns of "down island." I didn't know it then, but it was no accident she entered my life at this time. She would be a rock and comfort for me in the months and years to follow. The beginning of the preparation for the biggest fight of my life. Funny that, how when you look back at life you start to notice people entering and exiting the stage at such key times that there's no way it could be "random."

In the fall, I decided to commute to Brooklyn for prenatal yoga training. That was the most intense teacher training. I felt like I was studying to be an OBGYN. I had a lot of experience, being a registered nurse and having five children. I thought this training would round out my teaching. I considered being a labor doula, an add on from my earlier nursing career. I had never heard of that position until the prenatal training. A doula is a trained, non-medical, emotional, physical and educational support system for the expecting mom. I was never offered that type of assistance while in labor. The doula also intercedes in the birthing process with the midwife or hospital staff while the mom can't speak because she is in so much pain! I could have gone down that path, but I decided against it. Babies are unpredictable, they come whenever they want. My first hospital job as a nurse was the night shift in the nursery. I realized I needed a more certain schedule, waking up to go to work at two in the morning when someone's water broke wasn't my style.

When we closed our sessions during the prenatal training, we would gather in a circle. I spent a lot of time in circles. If we wanted to talk, we would pick up the pelvis bone that was in the middle and hold it like a talking stick. I laughed to myself holding the pelvis as I thought of the size of Jack's head and body when he was born—weighing in at eleven and three-quarter pounds. All my kids were over ten pounds, but he was the biggest. Right after he was born, when I asked Kevin how Jack was doing in the nursery, he said, "He's on the phone ordering a pizza."

My yoga community is a core support for me on my life journey. More and more my friends and acquaintances began to speak the same language. We were all on the same journey, one of self discovery. Deepening our understanding of self, through self, not from the external but from the internal. "It's an inside job," Sherry would say, and no one can do it for us. We are each our own guru, our own healer. Well, that all sounds good, except I ended up with high blood pressure, extra weight, and out of control stress. Where were the teachings?

I decided yoga wasn't enough to get me into the shape I wanted to be. I don't think of yoga as exercise any longer. I added on personal training and boxing. I mean boxing in the ring, with the sweetest man ever. I would arrive at the gym, jump on the treadmill for a mile run, and cry to him as I ran. Working out and crying went together for me. So much sadness. I could share Jack's journey with my friend and trainer. He was no stranger to drugs and jail. He had a cousin with the same issues.

I also shared my divorce traumas. He was a good listener.

After I finished my warm up, we would get in the ring and throw down some punches following the strengthening portion of the work out. Hook, cross, upper cut. All three of my boys went to my sessions on different occasions, which made me happy. I added on Pilates reformer. After all that, I still wasn't in any shape?

It wasn't really about shape, I don't think. It was about surviving what was about to happen. The levels of durability from all the different trainings is why I am still standing today.

The "who am I, where am I, what am I doing" was thrown into complete chaos for years. First, trying to get divorced for years while my husband was gallivanting around in our community, yet he would not comply with the divorce process. Then Jack spinning out of control. More (many more) than once did I think of driving my car off the road. It was too much to bear, but I had to persevere. I needed crazy out of my life. It had to be Kevin, my husband who went first. I had to get on my feet. It took four years, two lawyers, and tons of money to make that happen. I knew I needed to focus on me, Jack and my other children then.

The divorce was finalized on March 15, 2015. I had to go on the witness stand, which no one told me about beforehand. I was so afraid. I could barely say my name. I cried through the entire process. When it was over, I ran from the courthouse and didn't look back.

Jack had not yet left for Cali where he was residing at the time. He said, "So the divorce is final?"

"Yes it is," I replied.

"Congratulations," he said.

I didn't feel as though it was worth congratulating. It was the second saddest day of my life. I was barely divorced, still mourning my marriage, when the saddest day came, just two weeks later.

After Jack passed, I stopped my yoga teaching. I stopped going to yoga classes at the studio that I had attended every day of the week for years. Eventually, I did begin to practice again, at home, twenty minutes on my own, which I still do. My yoga practice became one of meditation and self-awareness. Working on my handstand and other arm balances became less important.

I am Barbara, on Martha's Vineyard, writing our book...

*February 7, 1997*

*My Jackamo,*

*My special angel from God. You fill me with so much Joy. So much time has passed. I'm not very good at keeping up with my journal, you boys don't give me a second to rest. I don't even know where to begin. I guess last summer...*

*Well, you took your training wheels off your bike and rode off into the sunset. Spending the summer at the pool, jumping off the diving board, doing flips off the side. Wait, let me remind you, my little monkey, that you are two and a half years old. You were also in tennis lessons. This summer you won a blue ribbon in the 4th of July three and under foot race and we also received a blue ribbon for our Olympic Float.*

*In September, you started nursery school in Mrs. Carlson's class. It started small but it's getting bigger. You are a sweet heart in class and you follow all the directions. You have lots of buddies and have play dates with them.*

*This summer you went to Martha's Vineyard. Samara and James (your nannies) have been teaching you lots of Spanish words. You love to cook and bake. You especially love pancakes.*

*At night you love to sleep with "My Spot." He is so snuggly. You love horses and your farm set. This fall you rode Pumpkin the pony.*

*You love to go to Papa's farm. That is when we told you we were having another baby. You are such a loving big brother to Henry. You call him, affectionately, "Hen." He loves you, too. Willie loves you so much. You guys get crazy a lot and someone always gets hurt. You are always playing with the big boys. You love Kenny and Robert and play with them all the time.*

*For Halloween, you were Superman. You were sooo cute. I love your little body! Especially your snuggly bottom. You will end up driving the girls crazy. Boy, will I have my hands full with you and your handsome brothers, breaking hearts.*

*For Christmas Santa brought you a new bike, along with so many toys. All our family came over for dinner. We had our annual New Year's Eve party and kids were everywhere.*

*Two weeks ago we went to Mt. Snow. I said when you learned to stop you could go on the chair lift. Well, it didn't take long at all and you were skiing with me, Daddy and Willie. Next week we are going to visit Nonie and Pops in Florida and after that we will be on vacation in Nevis. Then, we come back and our new baby will be coming. We are very busy. I can't wait to be home from work so we can be together.*

*Your birthday is late, in September. You always want to know when it will be your birthday.*

*I am on a plane right now and it is getting a wee bit bumpy.*

*Auntie Linda and Uncle Rob are having a baby too, in April. I'm due May 1st. Jack Conroy, you have the sweetest wee voice, I love it. You call your aunties Uncle Lelly and Uncle Cathy.*

*You have so much love and kindness in your heart. I pray for your life of love and laughter, friends and family. You are a treasure, God has blessed me and you. I pray for God to always watch over you as I know he will and has already done. Thank you God for Jack.*

*I love you with all my heart and more.*

*Love today and always, mommy xoxoxox*

*Little Jackamo*

# IT TAKES A VILLAGE

School, let's just say, wasn't really Jack's thing. Starting out in the church nursery school, I'll never forget it. Things were going fine until Halloween. He was full of energy to dress up and trick or treat. He was going as Superman. In preparation, he would fly around and around the kitchen counter in his costume, so excited. Halloween finally came and it was time to wear his costume to school. Being members of the church and attending Sunday school, we were all very comfortable with the surroundings, the staff and the other children. I was holding Jack's hand as he flew through the door and down the hall.

When we entered the classroom, the teacher looked at Jack's costume and pulled me aside. She said the children were not permitted to dress up in school. I'm thinking, what the heck? Do you think dressing like Superman is some kind of devil worship? This was not okay. We were supposed to leave a change of clothes in the classroom in case of accidents and the teacher asked that I change him into those and out of his costume.

No, I was not doing that. I was not going to disappoint my little boy. He was so excited about his costume. I picked him up and walked out. We decided to trick or treat early that year. I was so mad that I took him out of the school, my church, and signed him up for the nursery school in town. They sang all kinds of songs there, and celebrated fun events, including Halloween.

The incident with the church preschool was only the beginning of the trouble to come. Jack went to elementary school with his big brother, Willie. They rode the bus together. I sent Jack off with his own lunch box and backpack just like the big boys had. Shorts and Velcro sneakers all ready to go. He loved his sneakers; he wore Vans later on. He was very particular. They had to be just the right color. His favorite were the dark green suede. Laces

*43*

had to be tied a very specific way. Yeah, Jack was a cool cat.

On his first day of elementary school, I followed behind the bus to meet him so when the bus arrived at school I could take him to meet his new teacher. Off the bus, the kids lined up at the door. "Keep feet, hands and all objects to yourself." That was the rule, although it never was the case at home. Tackling, wrestling, pushing, those rules didn't seem to apply outside of school.

One day we received a call from the principal. Somehow Jack got his hands on bullet casings. Turns out he got them from Stefano, a little boy who lived in our neighborhood, Will's best friend. The casings were antiques. Jack showed them to a kid in his class, and then gave him one to keep. The kid brought it home and showed it to his parents, and it landed Jack in the principal's office. Bullets at school. Well, actually, they were bullet casings. It was a mistake, and we apologized to the boy's mom and the principal.

Jack the artist started to emerge. I didn't even realize how talented he was then. It started with the snowman picture. It won first prize for the most creative picture in class. He didn't even tell me. Someone else saw it hanging in the window of the town art center. I still have it. The black paper with the white snowman and all the snow falling around him. Jack said, "It's just a snowman." But the art teacher saw something there. It was his handwriting, too. Just like my dad, beautiful penmanship. His printing was perfect. He would even try to messy it up because he thought it looked like "girl handwriting." Silly Jackamo, it was a gift. I have his graffiti name on tables, computers, TVs, basketballs, he would write it everywhere...JACKSON.

St. Luke's started in the fifth grade and went through twelfth. Kevin and I decided this was the place for our children to get the best education. We chose it for the small class sizes and the special care each student would receive from their teachers. Will was already enrolled there. Now it was Jack's turn. He immediately made lots of friends and joined all the sports teams. He was an incredible athlete, naturally gifted at football, lacrosse, soccer and basketball. He was a star player right from the start. Well, well before middle school. He had been playing soccer since he was four, along with T-ball, hockey, swimming and diving, snowboarding, and skiing. It didn't matter what it was; if it was physical, he was good at it.

There were loads of extracurricular activities at St. Luke's and fun class trips. The first big one was to Gettysburg in the sixth grade. It was a two-night trip and the entire class went. Not long into the trip we got the call from the chaperone. Jack stepped on a stink bomb on the bus and everyone had to get off and stay out until it cleared up. Stink bombs can clear a room. When exploded, they emit a very unpleasant odor. Some students were even dizzy and nauseous. Jack said it was his friend Theo's and that he just stepped on it, but I'm not certain about that.

By eighth grade, Jack played on all the varsity teams. Sports were Jack's thing. His real support came from his coaches. They always had his back. Most of the teachers did too, except for that one crazy chemistry teacher in ninth grade. He and Jack just didn't get along. He picked on Jack, on everything he did.

At the end of the year, the head master called us in for a meeting. He felt it would be better for Jack if he didn't return to St. Luke's for the tenth grade. The classes would be getting more demanding and he thought Jack would not be able to keep up with the work. I didn't understand. He did well in English and history. It was just chemistry. But Jack and this teacher had major conflicts. In the end, the teacher was fired, but not before he failed Jack. That head master only wanted perfect kids. My son was perfectly Jack.

Not returning to St. Luke's was fine with Jack. He didn't like the school anyway—too many rules. Brien McMahon High School was a mile up the road from our house. Jack's childhood friends were there, and they had a great lacrosse team. The lacrosse coach took Jack under his wing. Once again he found his place in sports. But changing schools was not the simple cure we hoped it would be. There were a set of challenges at McMahon also.

Thinking back on it, I never actually saw him do homework at home, or bring books to school. His backpack had a bottle of water and a bagel in it. I don't know if he went to class or not. McMahon was a big school, ten times the size of St. Luke's. Three or four middle schools fed into it. Jack said he could put his hood over his head and go to sleep on his desk during class. He couldn't even wear a hood at St. Luke's.

I tried to get acclimated to the new school and its systems. I didn't know many of the parents, and it was nothing like St. Luke's. The cafeteria at St.

Luke's had a fireplace, and chefs. Jack wouldn't eat the cafeteria food at McMahon, so I brought him lunch practically every day. Mostly from Subway but also from his favorite, Garden Catering. The High School Special, fried chicken and those little tater tots and their special seasoning, "extra please." Garden Catering was in Stamford, not right around the corner. I didn't mind the drive though, I'd do anything for my kids. Since he wasn't allowed out once school started, I would drive up and he would leave his sneaker in the door to run out and get his lunch, the hand-off.

I remember his first parent's night. I followed his class schedule and met all the teachers. One of the classes surprised me, African History. I was the only white parent in the class. That was cool though. Not sure they thought I was cool.

His music was all rap, and nasty. He would smoke weed in the morning and barely try to hide it. I would catch him almost every day. I said to him, "Jack, you know you're not black, right?" He would always talk N-word this and that. I thought it was just a phase.

His style was lax, too. Jack always wore sweatpants over a pair of lacrosse shorts and boxers, the sweatpants sliding down under his butt. I was constantly pulling them up and over his big round bottom. Just like when he was a baby. We started calling him Jack-a-bum.

At the same time, he loved preppy clothes. Vineyard Vines took up a lot of his closet. Also some finer things, like cashmere sweaters and scarfs. Specific colors weren't for him, certain styles too. It had to be just right—Jack style.

Some days when I dropped him at school, on the way to take Henry and Grace to St. Luke's, I would see him walk right back out the door in the rearview mirror. I would whip around to try to get him back in the building. One time I dropped him off and headed back home, a mile away. I entered the house and the phone rang. I hate the phone. It was Jack's advisor, this enormous black man with black eyes to match. He scared the shit out of me. "Come pick Jack up, he's been smoking marijuana, and he is suspended." What? I left him there five minutes ago. Damn! Suspended again.

I videotaped all of Jack's games and cheered him on. He would put black war paint under his eyes before the games. I think it was supposed to reflect the sun, but if he was running at me with a stick in his hand, I would definitely run in the other direction. Jack, Scott, Connor, Mike, Issac and Oliver, great friends, great coach and team. Seemed like they had lots of fun together. The team dinners were at Outback Steak House, not the New Canaan Country Club like at St. Luke's. We liked it though.

I edited the video footage I had taken of Jack's games and put together a DVD to send to schools for Jack. It was time for college, but I didn't even know if Jack was going to graduate high school. I filled out the applications myself and sent the DVD's to coaches. I should have left it alone, but Jack's coach called and said the coach at Endicott College wanted to meet Jack. His friends Connor and Scott would both be attending and be on the team.

We drove up past Boston to Beverly, Massachusetts. Jack looked so handsome in his blazer and nice hair cut. We waited in the elegantly decorated lobby. It was a beautiful old school, originally a girl's school, right on the Atlantic Ocean. Perfect for Jack, as he loved the water. There were big old stone buildings and a beautiful lake in front on the quad with a little bridge over it. Great looking kids hurrying off to class or to the library. The cafeteria had salad stations, pizza stations, and more.

The president of the school and the coach came out to greet us. When Jack stood up and shook their hands, I was so proud of him. They were immediately impressed by his size and confidence. He had such poise, and charm. Big handshake, "Look right in their eyes," I taught my kids, worked every time. They accepted Jack for the fall.

College didn't go so well. School just wasn't Jack's thing. He never played lacrosse and spent the year avoiding the coach. I believe, but am not entirely sure, that this is when the pills started. I know Jack took Scott's Klonopin, I think that was the beginning. He didn't return to Endicott the next year. We decided a three-month trip to NOLS (National Outdoor Leadership Program) would be best.

*Jack's senior year playing attack on the McMahon Lacrosse Team*

*November 12, 1998*

*Dear Jackamo,*

*My little Kindergardian. What a big boy you are. You are a happy guy, nice to everyone (but when you get mad, although not often, you get really mad.)*

*You have a happy face, you're always the first to say OK. You want to do everything.*

*You are an incredible athlete, bikes, rollerblades, ice skating, skiing, soccer, swimming, you name it, you can do it.*

*Over the summer on Martha's Vineyard you were riding the waves.*

*Now, the 1ˢᵗ day of school. You were nervous sweet boy, you took the bus with Willie, I met you when you got off and brought you straight to Mrs. Arndt's class. She says you are doing great at school, learning your letters with your word cards. I'm so happy for you. You have nice friends, but you love Robert and Kenny.*

*I'm far away from you right now, sweet pea. I'm on a plane flying over Africa, it's a long way from home.*

*Tomorrow, I'm going to surprise you and pick you up from your class. I can't wait to give you a hug!*

*Where I've been Jack is Sri Lanka and Indonesia. There are so many starving. No food to eat. Pray for them, sweet boy. God has blessed us in so many ways. I pray he is watching over you now while you sleep.*

*I love you, mommy xo hugs and kisses.*

*February, 12, 2002*

*Dear Jackie,*

*My little blasternaut. How is it, sweet boy, that you can't walk into a room, you blast into a room. You have so much energy, you can't sit still.*

*It's Henry's birthday!!!*

*You are a sweet boy, everybody loves Jack. But be still, be calm, God loves you, be quiet, there is time. You have so many emotions just now. Let's be still and understand what is happening in your life. You are doing nicely at school. You always are trying to be with Will's friends though. Jack Henson is your buddy and so much like you. How great to have such a nice friend.*

*You are a wonderful athlete. Good and agile at everything. Snowboarding, skate boarding, roller blading, soccer, baseball, basketball. You name it, you are good at it, and also a good sport. Unless, that is, if you have a JACK ATTACK! AHHH!!! Self control sweet boy. Be calm and still.*

*It has been a different year. September 11 changed our lives. We lost a dear friend in Andrew King and feel so sad for our friends.*

*I love you so much. Always honor God. Be kind and respectful of others, "Be still and know that I am God."*

*I love you Jackie.*

*Love mommy  xoxoxo*

*June 26, 2009*

*Dear Jack,*

*I am having difficulty finding the words to capture the feelings I have. I struggle to find you in all the behaviors that surround you.*

*I know you in your soul, mothers know. I know that the gifts you have been blessed with include strength and beauty, agility, deep goodness, compassion, wisdom, and an uncanny ability to figure things out. These qualities that are true to your soul have been overshadowed by behaviors that are dark, like a cloud that covers the best of you.*

*I have come to believe that this is something you are unable to control, a series of behaviors that don't fit in this home and world that we live in. Typically you would say, "it is no big deal, I am sorry. I am so annoying." Say it if you want, but this behavior has gone too far.*

*I believe trust is the greatest virtue. I have lost trust in you. Not only do you lie but it happens constantly. You seem not to have any guilt for it either which is frightening. I fear for you and for me.*

*These behavioral problems that include talking back, failing in school, being disrespecting with us, your siblings, and your teachers, topped with drinking, smoking, lying and now stealing have left us no choice but to seek other measures. Turning off a cell phone or keeping you from an activity are far from the necessary disciplines needed for you to live a healthy and prosperous life.*

*I am profoundly sad and afraid. You have so much to offer and are capable of great things. You will not reach your potential following the path of destruction that you are choosing.*

*We will be speaking to you about your options as we discuss them with professional assistance.*

*I love you*

*Faces, Anger, Saddness, Lonliness, and Worry*

## COPS AND ROBBERS

I always felt that if Denzel Washington lived in my house, packing a side arm, life would have been a lot different. Some bad ass, with a gun, yeah, that would have worked. The teenage years were tough. Starting with Will, the pot smoking! Now it's legal, but then I spent so much time as the cop in my home. Then came Jack. Will said he and Jack used to smoke when Jack was very young, maybe thirteen. I know he feels like he helped Jack start down this path, but he was not responsible for the outcome. We all have so much guilt.

Jack was fifteen at the end of August 2009. It would be two weeks before he turned sixteen and could apply for his permit. He needed to get legal. I was certain he took my car at night, Will too. I slept with my keys, but somehow, it would be the night I forgot, or he found the spare.

Kevin finally left for rehab. He had been going down hill since the financial crisis in 2008. He catastrophized every event that fall. This led to endless days in bed, not taking care of his responsibilities, including work and family. Everything fell on me. It became overwhelming, taking care of the kids, working full time, and having a husband in bed. With family support, Kevin admitted himself to a rehabilitation program for depression.

Phew! He was out of the house and getting the necessary help to bring himself back to life. I felt relieved.

It was a rainy night, and I went to bed early like I always do. Kevin was safe, it was going to be all right.

"Jack, you scared me, what's up?"

"Mom, I did something really bad."

"Tell me," I said.

Jack was afraid and crying at my bedside. I didn't know what had happened. I sat up and three police cars with sirens came around the block. In front of them was a white SUV.

"Mom, I took the Jeep to drive Scott home, it slipped out on a puddle and I landed on someone's stone wall."

"Were you drinking?"

"No," he said.

He was afraid. Kevin was gone. We headed for the front door. Will, Jack and I greeted the police. They asked for Jack's license, but he didn't have one because he was fifteen. They cuffed his hands behind his back in front of me and took him away.

When the police are involved, I get a feeling of helplessness. Aren't they supposed to be helpful? I was so scared they were taking Jack away from me. There was nothing I could do. I had to let him go. Will and I waited up until two in the morning figuring out how to get bail money. We got him out and back to safety at home.

I immediately found a lawyer who dealt with adolescent cases. Jack was underage, and the charge would eventually be expunged. He had to do community service and was on probation, as well as get drug tested regularly.

Twice a week Jack had to attend an adolescent recovery group in the next town. I drove him after school and waited in the parking lot. The facilitator said Jack was participating, his urine was clean, and she had high hopes for his success.

That winter, maybe around the Christmas dance, came the beer throwing incident. Jack had had a girlfriend but they had recently broken up. Jack, more than his brothers, always had a girl on his arm.

We found out later that she didn't approve of Jack's behavior, the drinking and smoking. She ended up with a lacrosse team member of Jack's, not Jack. At the party, Jack was drinking. He saw this teammate with his now ex-girlfriend and threw a beer can. It hit the kid on his neck underneath his ear.

Not good.

The boy was stitched up. The doctor told the family that had it been any lower, the can would have cut the carotid artery. The family pressed charges, and we were back at the lawyers. I can't even remember what the punishment was this time, probation I am sure, anger management of some kind. Drug testing again. Our lawyer tried the tough guy approach, trying to scare Jack with jail, what would happen to him inside. It didn't work on Jack, but I was petrified.

The legal issues were starting to accumulate. Jack had to report to his probation officer regularly and get drug tested. He always passed. He had a "wizinator," a fake penis he tied to his leg. I am not sure where he got the urine, or if it came with the kit. So ridiculous but he never got caught.

Despite my warnings, Jack did what ever he wanted, always living on the edge. He never seemed to be afraid of getting caught. I purchased a security system. It was not to keep unwanted guests from getting in, it was to keep Jack from going out. It didn't work. He disabled it. He was so freak'n clever.

Jack could do anything. He was big and strong, smart and resourceful. I asked a lot of him, particularly when Kevin left the house. Whether it was random chores, heavy lifting, or grilling. He was excellent on the grill, leaving it spotless after he used it. The perfect clean. He also loved to bake. I can still see him making a Betty Crocker cake from the mix and frosting it, enjoying eating it with Grace or friends. He would always say to me, "Mom, why do I have to do everything?" And I would reply, "Because you can."

The following summer Jack and his buddies took the Metro North train to Stamford for a summer concert series called "Live at Five." Great bands, good crowds, always seemed to be fun for everyone. Well, on this particular night, I guess there was too much fun going on. Jack and his friends had been drinking during the concert. Apparently, they were getting rowdy on the train home, banging the sides, disturbing passengers. By the time they arrived at the station, the cops were there to greet them and assess the situation.

While the police had one of the guys face down to cuff him, Jack decided to run away from the scene and get himself home to bed. He knew if he were arrested again it would mean big trouble, probably jail. Will came home that night and told me he heard there was a warrant out for Jack's arrest. Again. Kevin got involved and they went to the police station, where Jack turned himself in. Whenever I was in my house and saw a police car drive around the block, I would be texting Jack, "Where are you? The cops are around the house." I didn't know if they were looking for him, or if it was just an ordinary patrol, but I was afraid all the time.

One night, I woke up to lights shining in the front of the house. Jack wasn't even home, he was staying with his dad. I looked out my bedroom window to see three police cars with lights blaring. Oh my God, what is going on now? Jack staying at Kevin's was better for me, Grace and Henry. It was calmer without him at home. Heart pounding, I answered the door, immediately thinking something happened to Jack. But thankfully, that was not the problem. The alarm was going off at the restaurant we own in town and Kevin wasn't picking up his phone, so they came to the house. I called Jack's cell and he picked up and woke Kevin. I nearly had a heart attack when I saw the cars. Police were supposed to protect us, but after all we'd been through with them and Jack, they scared me to death.

When I asked Kevin for a divorce and he left the house, it happened to be near the time when my car lease was up. I needed to decide what kind of new look I was going for. Well, I made an emotional purchase for sure and bought a new Porsche Cayenne S, black of course.

Yes, I felt empowered. I had a bad ass car. It looked cool, it was fast, but was crazy expensive and terrible on gas. What a dumb idea. I drove it around feeling cool though for a couple of years. The car became more and more popular, and I began to see it on every corner when I pulled up to stop. Then I saw women I didn't like with my same car. Okay, no. This car had to go.

I decided to go with something a little different, a vehicle where I could be transparent. I opted for a 2014 Black Ford 150 pickup. Yup! No one would recognize me. I even had it registered in Massachusetts to complete the disguise.

The night before the Porsche was due to be turned in and I would be picking up my new truck, Jack borrowed the car. He said he was going to a doctor twenty minutes away that was helping him with his drug problem. I let him drive my car, on its last day with me.

Jack called about an hour later saying the coolant light was flashing and the car was heating up. I told him to stay with the car, do not drive it and call AAA. An hour later, he was back at the house. Now I had a problem. I was turning the car in the next day, I was receiving a check from Ford for the Porsche for ten thousand dollars, and I had lights flashing all over the dashboard. Jack told me to get coolant and a funnel and to meet at my house and he would help me with the procedure. Always helpful, resourceful, my Jack.

I got a call from Grace, who forgot her lacrosse stick at home and needed it for practice after school. I texted Jack that I would meet him later instead. Driving down the road I saw Jack and his buddies. He rolled down the window and said he would take the stick to Grace. I thanked him, but no, I was already on my way. I would see him at the house in about an hour.

On the way to school, I saw several police cars and some kids up against the sides. I slowed down to see if I knew any of them, maybe classmates of Grace or Henry's? But drove on. After delivering the stick to Grace, I headed home. I got a text from one of my yoga students. She was an artist and worked at the Rowayton Arts Center, where Jack's snowman picture had hung so many years before. Her text read, "Cops just arrested Jack outside the art center." She sent me her brother's information; he was a lawyer.

How could this be? I thought. I just saw him, he was in good spirits, he was going to meet me. What the hell is going on?

Ten Darien cops arrested Jack in the middle of town. Everyone was out of their shops and watching this take place. They grabbed him and he tried to run. Really? Did he really think he was going to get away? They had him on the street and cuffed him behind his back. That was my son, for God's sake, he must have been so afraid. Or not.

He was set up. An undercover cop met him at the Rowayton Market to buy Adderall. The Adderall was a prescription that he got from the fucking doctor the night before. They took him in.

Somehow, he turned in another kid in Darien, and they let him go. What is completely crazy is that the Darien cops don't have jurisdiction in Norwalk, so they had no right arresting him. You would think they would have thought that through before sending ten cars into town.

It was still time to turn in my car. I couldn't even think straight. What if they didn't take it because of all the lights blinking? I had to get it traded in, I needed that $10,000 check. I went to the car, placed the funnel where I thought it should go and poured the coolant in. It poured right out. There was a gaping hole in the pipe.

I needed to get this car to Norwalk. I gave up on the coolant and jumped in. Speeding up the Bluff Hill, all lights blinked in red. I smelled smoke. I turned off the car and rolled to the stop light. There was construction all the way and it took forever. Every traffic light I came up against was red. Time to turn off the car and cool down. I did this for twenty minutes until I saw the McMahon Ford sign. Oh my God, I was going to make it. I was shaking like a leaf. My car was about to explode, my son just got arrested in our little two horse town, and I just needed to get this car traded in. Oh shit, I realized I scheduled my annual physical for today, too. What was I thinking? There was way too much going on.

I pulled up alongside the dealership, turned off the car and waited for the smoke to stop. I took about fifteen minutes to compose myself and then I walked in.

"I'm here to pick up my new truck."

My heart was racing, abnormally for sure. I signed some paperwork, and the salesman took out the check and my new keys. I tried to steady my hands as I reached for them both. He went on and on about this and that, I don't even know what he said. Just give me the fucking check and keys. Finally, I had them. We walked to the truck. I hopped in and so did he. He began to explain all the features of the vehicle. I said, "Look, I am in a real hurry, I will look it up in the manual." One step left, he needed to remove my license plates from the Porsche and give them to me to return to the DMV. Bent over at the back of the car he fumbled with the screwdriver. He couldn't unscrew the plates! Now what? He said he needed to drive the Porsche around to service and they would do it. OH NO! As soon as he turned on the car, he would see all the lights flashing on the dashboard. He got in the car. I watched in the rear view mirror. He pulled out and gunned it around me and around the corner to service. It was a cool car for sure, and super fast, so he was probably taking a test drive. I thought the car was going to blow up! When he came back, he didn't say anything about the Porsche. He handed me the plates and I bolted from the scene. Somehow I'd made it out! That was intense. Now for the doctor's appointment.

On the highway I realized the size of my new truck. I was unsteady, in a new car, my heart was still racing which was making me dizzy, this could not be safe. I arrived at the doctor's office and they took my blood pressure. One eighty over one hundred. She took it again. I said, "No that makes sense." My resting heart rate was one hundred and twenty four.

The doctor came in and I burst into tears.

*April 19, 2012*

    *I am in disbelief at your exit back to school. I don't even feel like writing because nothing changes. It is the same repetitive behavior, disrespect beyond words, verbal abuse and lies.*

    *You have everything and your response is the same. Ungrateful, entitled, and I can't even think of a word to describe your bursts of anger.*

    *You convinced us you needed a car at school to look for work. That was a lie. Instead you took pills and flunked your classes. You stole from me again, $2,500.00. You took my credit card without permission.*

    *Every time you call me and want money to fill your gas tank or whatever, I do it. I give you your allowance early. You came home to work, as if you deserve a job. You repeatedly blow off anything that is set up for you. You had an opportunity to work at Grasso Construction, you blew them off. You were completely capable of working. You bullshitted the doctor about your knee pain from the ACL injury, tried to get pills, but he suggested Tylenol and a knee brace, which you never were going to wear, but I paid for it anyway.*

    *You said you would paint the fence around the house to reduce your most recent debt, but instead you took pills (which you said you didn't take) that left you passed out for the day and the debt unpaid. You said Henry said you could take his car, he did not. You did nothing about your car, I called and got it towed, I called to take care of the problem, it needs a new gear shift which is $1,300.00. Who's paying for that? Me.*

    *I don't care how you feel about Dad, you do not speak to any human being like that.*

    *You had everything all wrong anyway. I told you Dad was coming with the appraiser. He did not come to check on you. I called the house to make sure you were at the dentist, and of course you blew that off too because you were passed out on the sofa. That is twice, I will not make another appointment for you. Your teeth will rot and your wisdom teeth will be impacted. You will be off our insurance by the time the pain will start.*

*I don't know what is wrong with you, but it is bad!*

*Thank you for picking up my charger at Apple and painting a little and getting my furniture and taking care of Lakeview.*

*So you're pissed off because I took your pills. I don't care, it is my job to protect you from harm. If you got behind the wheel (which you did) you could have killed yourself or someone else.*

*I don't want a response.*

*Art Journal page, Tears*

# BRASS KNUCKLES

I don't know how we ever got to this point. Kevin and I were separated, and he had been out of the house for nearly six months. It was a very difficult time. Jack did not follow any rules I set. I wrote them down, had him sign contracts. None of it mattered. It seems vague at this point, for which I am glad. It's like not remembering how painful it was to give birth and you do it again, and in my case again and again and again.

The same with Kevin, again and again and again. I thought we had the perfect life, despite the bumps. Opposites attract, right? No, like attracts like, I messed that up. Like minded people are attracted to one another. That was why all my friends and I spoke the same language. It all seemed great, love, family, friends, job, beautiful home, charming community. Jack had a few issues to work out, but I knew he would work them out eventually. So what was I missing? Even with our big beautiful life, something still wasn't right. I was so caught up in my own whirlwind life I guess I overlooked some things. A lot of things. The details are insignificant. I don't want to talk about it.

We were still living together when one day I received an anonymous email that blew up the perfect illusion I thought of as my life. My perfect life wasn't so perfect after all. It's funny, well not funny, but looking back, knowing all I know now, it still doesn't change how I look at our life together. My reality then was we had built an amazing life, it was my perception.

My husband continued with unusual behavior in and out of the house. Late nights, no shows, nothing ever seemed to add up. Being on shifting sand left me with this terrible feeling in my gut. I should have listened to my intuition, but it was so covered up with fear, which I identified later. I didn't know it was fear, it was not a feeling I recognized or understood. But it was fear. It was very tough on all of us. Kevin's relationship with our kids was very strained, and even more strained with me.

I left with Grace and Henry for Martha's Vineyard for the summer, in July 2013. This time without Kevin, Will, and Jack. We have a darling cottage in the seafaring village called Menemsha. It is a simple, beautiful space, and I needed it badly. Will stayed at home to attend a therapeutic program for some emotional strain he had experienced. Jack had to go to summer school. Kevin stayed with the boys. The idea was for the three of them to spend the summer together rebuilding a broken relationship with a counselor facilitating their journey. I told Kevin when I left that when I returned, if things did not change with his behavior, he needed to leave our home. I was hoping for a positive change on my return. We needed Kevin back as my husband and a good father, like it used to be.

Martha's Vineyard is the place for healing. The beautiful ocean, vineyards rambling along the road side, feet in the sand, and yoga. Grace did her riding (she started pony camp at age four and has been riding ever since, a very accomplished equestrian), and worked at Pond View Farm. Henry worked at The Galley, a take-out place right down the road from our cottage in Menemsha, making shakes, or frappes, rather. He was convinced he wanted a desk job with a computer and air conditioning in the future.

At the end of the summer, Grace and I left the island with her horse, JD, to attend a horse show on Cape Cod. From there, our plan was to head home from summer fun back to school for her, and back to the rest of the family. Her first round went great and she was waiting to go in for her next round. JD—On Call was his show name—was a sweet horse, tall and lean. Grace rode in the hunter division and equitation. In these divisions, the rider is judged on her and the horse's performance as a whole. Polished boots, perfect seat on the horse, heels down, shoulders back, the correct number of strides to the jump. She always won.

Grace and I spent a lot of time at the barn. Jack used to love to ride too. He rode this little pony named Pumpkin and also a big white horse named Willie. He was supposed to walk and trot around, but turn your back for a second and he was cantering around the ring. I love horses. Their presence and size makes you realize their power, a power greater than ours.

My phone rang. Oh God. It was my sister, Leslie. She told me my dad was dying. My dad had been sick for a while with dementia, and cancer of the bladder. The hospice nurse said based on his breathing, he only had hours to live.

I was so far away, Grace was just about to go in the ring, and my sister said, "You need to come now." I called Kevin, and he and the boys headed to the farm where my parents lived in Bucks County, Pennsylvania. I called Grace over and told her I had to leave, Papa was dying. She was so sad, a big tear dropped from under her helmet, but I left. I drove eighty plus miles per hour to get from Cape Cod to the farm in record time, but I didn't make it. I was stuck in traffic on the Tappan Zee Bridge. Will told him I loved him.

Grace recently told me how sad she was that I left her while her family was all by Papa's side. I am so sorry about that. I couldn't make those split second decisions as well as Jack. He was so good under pressure. Me, not so much.

The farm, a special place. My mom and dad retired there. A gorgeous two-hundred acre estate with a two-hundred-year-old farm house and barn. The hills reminded my parents of their homeland, the borders of Scotland. That is where they fell in love and were married before they came to the United States on the Queen Mary for their honeymoon. Scotland feels like home to me, too.

When I arrived at the farm, my family came to me. They all had the opportunity to say goodbye, but I didn't. Kevin said, "I got the boys here" several times. "Why is this about you?" I thought. Nothing about me, my grief, my pain. I knew then nothing had changed. This relationship didn't serve me anymore. But I had to go and see my dad and say my goodbyes.

My plan for having a counselor work with Kevin, Will and Jack did not have a successful outcome. Jack was a junior in high school and he was in trouble. He was smoking weed all the time and had no respect for himself, his family, his home, his teachers or the law. He was out of control. He would sneak out of the house when I went to bed. I was always suspicious of cars that drove around my neighborhood. Seeing them coming around the side of my house, I would move from window to window to see if I recognized the driver. Most times I didn't.

I tried to keep things as stable as I could with the other kids. Henry and Grace were responsible and taking care of their schoolwork and sports. Grace was riding. Will was home for a semester and getting ready to head out to Berklee College of Music in Boston. The friction between Will and Jack was palpable. Will felt that Jack did not show him the respect due an older brother as they entered their teens. I don't know when it all switched, they were best buddies when they were little. I tried my best. I have been reminded that I did not give Henry and Grace the attention they needed and deserved. Will and Jack were the squeaky wheels.

In the middle of all that chaos, I had to tell my kids that I asked for a divorce and that their dad would be moving out. Of course, I had to be the one to tell them. Kevin was in denial and continuing his nothing short of crazy behavior. Coming into the house whenever he wanted, no boundaries, like it would all be okay. He would try to enforce discipline and no one would listen.

I told Will first. He said he had been anticipating this happening. I was so sorry. I then found Henry and Jack alone, I told them very quickly and they both dropped huge tears from their eyes, my big boys so sad. I had to do it, I felt paralyzed from my own personal growth. Kevin needed to do his own work, and I needed to do mine.

I told Grace alone, in the car. I felt enormous guilt. How could I do this to my children? Getting divorced went against every fiber of my being. Both Kevin's and my parents are still married, same with our siblings. Divorce wasn't a "thing" in our families. In my pain I could do nothing but blame. How could Kevin do this to his family?

During this time, Jack was completely out of control. He had been suspended from school. It was suggested I go to an "education specialist." Due to the violent outbursts, using weed daily, and slacking off in school, we realized we needed to take bigger steps. Kevin met me at the specialist's office. I was recently separated, my father had just died and this lady was telling me I had to send Jack to the Adirondacks for a year. Oh my God, my baby, what happened? I didn't want him to go. I was hysterical.

I warned Jack that this was being recommended. He was no dummy, he knew how it went down. I could see it already: he would struggle, unwilling to go, and a couple of big guys would put him in a van and take him away. I was devastated, I didn't want him to go, I just wanted him to stop.

In the morning, after the kids went to school, I would clean up and make the beds. One day I pulled back Jack's sheets and found them, brass knuckles. Shiny and paw-like. He was afraid. He was waiting for two men to take him away. I'm sorry you were scared, I was scared too.

I followed the recommendation. I had Jack packed with all the items from the list. The backpack was in the garage. We were two days away from Jack leaving.

Grace and I were upstairs watching TV together in one chair, probably *Pretty Little Liars*. Kevin came over, but I set up some boundaries. I wanted him to let me know in advance when he was coming to see the kids, and to knock at the door. It wasn't much to ask. I didn't mind that he came, as I would just go upstairs and do something else. I wanted Kevin to be with his children. All of a sudden, we heard yelling and rumbling downstairs, doors slamming. My heart stopped, the fear was back. Physical pain in my stomach and my chest. I ran down to see what was going on. Kevin and Jack got into it, and Jack ran out through the garage. He put his fist through the garage window and cut his wrist. Blood was spurting everywhere.

This was not entirely unusual in my home. A handshake quickly led to a wrap around the neck, to tackling to the floor, and then wrestling. I would be in the background yelling STOP! Someone always got hurt. I never understood this and still don't. We never behaved that way in my home when I was growing up.

Jack took his belt off and made a tourniquet around his arm. Seems like foreshadowing now. I wrapped his wrist with a towel and we headed to the Emergency Room.

It was bleeding a lot, so they took us right away. Jack was in a gown, lying on the gurney. I was sitting next to him with my head on his shoulder, crying. I was so scared. The doctor said he cut his tendons and needed deep stitches. He would need physical therapy for six months. The injury affected the motion he used as a star lacrosse player.

The Adirondack program wouldn't take him because there were so many physical demands. He was not going to go. Thank God!

April 8, 2009

Dear Jack,

I think talking to you is too difficult sometimes. I would like to remind you of a concept that you should tuck away in your heart. It is called respect. Respect runs through every aspect of your life.

Respect yourself, your mind, body, and soul. It is a gift, treat it so. Take care of your body, healthy food and water and exercise will sustain you. Feed your mind with good thoughts and education. Feed your soul with the love that is a gift from God just for you.

Respect your family. You KNOW how much we love you, we are just people trying to live the life we've been given. We deal with all the problems that come with life. We are not perfect but we try our best.

Respect your environment. Your/our home is where we all live. It is not by accident. We live here because of very hard work and it takes us all to keep it clean and happy.

Respect your education. It may seem meaningless to you, but it all has a purpose. You have all the capabilities to do well in school. If things were tough at times we had and have the resources to get you the help you needed. The world is a very complicated place. Someday you will need to provide for yourself and even others. You need to be educated or you will have trouble succeeding.

You will always reap what you sow. In other words, what you put into life you will get out in return. If one eats bad food, one will end up either fat or with disease. If one doesn't exercise one will be out of shape, if one smokes one will get disease. On the other hand if one works hard they have success, if one cares for others they will be taken care of. If one is respectful they are treated with respect.

Life is a journey, but everyday starts new. Every day we have the opportunity to make a change, make a turn in the direction of respect. *I pray for you today, and always that you turn and walk down the path of respect. It is in you, you are very fortunate to have the whole package...intelligence, health, resourcefulness, good looks and strength. You have the ability and knowledge to make good choices. But...you don't use the tools you have been given.*

*I hope you make the right choice about moving forward instead of quitting. About the right attitude. You owe it to yourself Jack.*

*I love you and I hurt. I know that was your intention and it worked. See, you do have the ability to make things happen!*

*Do your best Jack, you have never really seen all that you can do if you try your best. You will be presently surprised!!!!*

*mom*

*Menemsha River, Martha's Vinyard*

# HAPPY VINEYARD

I don't know what you saw. The gaze into the distant sea, something had your attention. Maybe it was the calling of the water which you loved so deeply, or maybe it was the warm sea breeze blowing your hair back off your face. Maybe it was the longing for calm and peace in your life, or maybe it was the longing for you to return home from once you came. Were you seeking a life of profound love and nothing more? Maybe it was your angel guide showing up for you as a reminder that there is a special place and that all will be well. Or maybe it was a hot girl in a bikini with a big butt.

Getting to this photo shoot was no easy feat. Now that they're all grown up with their own lives, getting all my kids together was more difficult. College, friends, work, all seemed to get in the way. Life got in the way. By the water we all feel at home. Menemsha, our happy place, where I was at home. Not sure my kids so much, they loved it too, but not like me. It was simple and comforting. The air is clean, the food is always fresh, and the people are my friends. I love Martha so much. I have had many futile attempts at hugging her waves, which left me in a self-embrace that I desperately needed.

Menemsha was where I chose to photograph my kids with a professional photographer in the summer of 2010. I needed to get some great shots. Will was twenty-one then, old enough to opt out of family photos from then on, so this was it, until I have grandchildren.

It was almost time to go down to the dock and meet the photographer, but before that, I told everyone to put on a solid shirt, no logos. Well, no one had that. Lacrosse jerseys, Dertbag hoodies, Island Music T's, nothing solid like I was instructed to bring but forgot. Will was late so I had to run down to the ferry and get him. I stopped at Midnight Farm, an eccentric clothing shop in one of the down island towns, Vineyard Haven, to see if they sold solid T's.

(Owned by Carly Simon, by the way.) Well, they did have what I was looking for, except the shirts were one hundred dollars each. There were two larges, but I needed an extra large for Jack. Jack was six-foot-four and super broad. There wasn't a solid one for him. I had to get one with a little writing, El Bait Shop it said. Jack loved to fish, so I got it.

He, of course, wanted to wear it inside out, so that was what was in all the photos, El Bait Shop, as he looked out to sea. Menemsha and Martha's Vineyard, yup, the perfect backdrop for my music loving, party crazy, studious, horseback riding, charismatic, amazing family. I love them so!

My husband wasn't there that summer. My Christmas card with my kids and only me confirmed that we were officially separated. I didn't want to be in the card, but the photographer convinced me. I loved it. Grace as usual was on Jack's lap, a separate love story and one that should be told. But his gaze, haunting actually. All the other kids looked right into the lens, but not Jack. They are handsome people. Kevin and I weren't so bad either; life just happened, and I wish it hadn't happened that way.

Summers on the Vineyard started when Henry was a baby. He would eat shells and sand on the beach. The big boys played in endless waves, a playground that never stopped. Our first family vacation to the island we stayed with my good friend Judy. Judy and I go way back. We met in Stowe, Vermont the year I finished college. I moved there with my boyfriend at the time and worked as a nurse at Mt. Mansfield. Judy had run away from home from the mainline of Philadelphia and was working multiple jobs. She lived above the funeral parlor in town, kind of creepy. Her windows were decorated with floral patterned balloon shades. I had never seen anything so beautiful. This girl had style. We became forever friends. Judy's husband Andrew died on September 11th. So much sadness, so much suffering.

Judy continued to winter in Stowe and summer on Martha's Vineyard. Time moved on, and we both got married, had kids. Judy invited us to visit her on the magical island of Martha. The large captain's house that she rented was on North Water Street in Edgartown. We could walk or bike to town to the shops and restaurants, it was adorable. We discovered the personalities of all the different communities on the island and fell in love with "up island." Rolling hills, endless moss-lined stone walls, side of the road farm stands, fresh fish daily, water everywhere, ocean, ponds, channels and streams. Judy preferred Edgartown.

We rented for years on Martha's Vineyard, many times with Judy and her family, falling more and more in love with the enchanted island. Then we found Menemsha. Menemsha felt like the original version of the town of Rowayton, where Kevin and I raised our family in Connecticut. Rowayton was once a small, humble fishing/lobster/oyster center on the coast of Connecticut. Kevin and I met and fell in love there. He was a fishmonger at the local lobster pound that later grew into an empire of sorts.

I loved how Rowayton used to be. I think we had something to do with its change of character, building a large beach home, opening a very successful seafood restaurant and gourmet market. Now Rowayton is an upscale, sought after, charming yet affluent community. Menemsha still feels quaint, original and unspoiled.

We loved it there so much we bought a cottage and renovated it with a special Conroy touch to make it an amazing retreat for us all. Chowder Kettle Lane could not have been more perfect. Bunks for the kids, screen doors that banged over and over again as one, two, three and many more headed out for capture the flag. I never quite understood the game, but it was played all the time there. Marshmallows charred outside on the fire, sunsets over the water that hundreds of tourists traveled up island to see—that faded to endless stars, galaxies, heavens, where does it all lead?

This tiny bungalow at the top of the drive held so many happy times. Lobster feasts were one of Jack's favorites. I made it every time he came. Steamers, mussels, oysters, corn, a proper New England lobster bake. It all happened at the kitchen table. For years we didn't have a TV, so the evening activities included chess, card games, those silly word games where you go around the table, like you learn at camp. I was notorious for messing them up, and my kids always let me know it.

Boats and fishing were and are popular with us. I always said we should use live bait, which worked every time, but the problem was we had to use eels. I remember a rainy day when Jack was in his early teens. We got on our bikes and headed down to the harbor with our bucket of eels and rods. Jack squeezed the eel's mouth and I dug the hook into its lips, disgusting! Now here was where we couldn't seem to agree on the details. Jack cast out the rod and passed it to me to prepare another, I hooked a striped bass and pulled it in. So, whose was it? Mine or his? I said it was mine. He said it was his. He caught many others on the beach, in the boat, on the dock. This one was mine, but I couldn't have done it without him.

Jack loved the boat. He was a master captain. He could dock Kevin's thirty-two foot Seavee (a sexy sport fishing boat) with two two-hundred-and-fifty horsepower Yamaha motors. Kevin taught all the kids how to manage the boat, but Jack could back the boat into the slip with his pinky finger on the levers. He would do it backwards, facing the motors. When the boat was in Connecticut, Jack and his friends would go below deck and smoke and drink. I would always find the evidence.

There are so many memories of boogie boarding, tubing (which with Kevin and the boys were always borderline dangerous), skim boarding, body boarding, castle building, soccer playing fun. Endless fun. "Happy Vineyard!" we would say. Simple activities escalated to shark fishing, surfboarding, and driving.

At ten years old, Jack loaded the kids on the lane into our little white Jeep with a stick shift, the top down. The neighbors' kids were five and seven and my kids were too. They were all hanging out of the car, no seat belts. Jack, behind the wheel, took off down the lane towards the road. Everyone was shouting and laughing, hands waving in the air, then the brakes gave out. All the kids started screaming, parents too. Jack turned a quick right and headed into the brush and the car stopped. Seriously, he could have driven all the kids into the road and God knows what would have happened. He could make split second decisions. At ten?

That's what it was like in Jack's life. Always, on the edge, and most times over the edge. It's where he lived.

Year after year the stakes got higher. Smoking started. Drinking started. Jack always hung with the big kids, Will and his friends. He would crawl in the window to the bunk room as late as four in the morning and tell me he was there all along, as I sat on the stairs and listened to the break in and surprisingly quiet retreat to his top bunk. The next day, he denied that he was out, said he had been snuggled in his bed all along.

How was it that we sat down to dinner in town in Edgartown—Jack, at seventeen years old, begging for a beer—ate dinner with friends, and the very next day I find a ticket in his pocket with the time and date listed on the top. He received a summons literally five minutes after he left the restaurant. He jumped in a car with a kid who had a tail light out, got pulled over with beer in the car, same old story, on the edge, caught again.

The next summer Jack didn't come to the Vineyard at all.

*Menemsha Beach family photo shoot, Summer 2011*

February 5, 2013

Dear Jack,

    I am picking up the bloody pieces of our family as once again, your toxic behavior has left us destroyed. I have re-read the countless letters that start the same way, Dear Jack. The desperate pleas to help you to get your life under control. The desperate pleas to follow the rules of our home, the desperate pleas to stop the drug use, the desperate pleas to respect yourself and your family and home, all falling on deaf ears. And there are the countless letters, Dear Jack, that outlined formulas for success and healthy living.

    The countless hours, days, weeks, years we have put up with your disrespect for any authority or respect for feelings and possessions of people who love you. The countless hours I spent driving you to counselors, drug testing, and court. The countless nights I spent awake worrying and being afraid of your temper and rage. Having to call the police as you threatened Henry or the fear after you put your hand through the glass. The time I/we have lost caught up in your crazy vortex is time we will never get back.

    I have been and still am desperate for your life to change, but it is out of my hands. There is zero trust, our relationship and that of your family and friends, shattered. I told you if you steal from me again our relationship is over. I told you repeatedly that if your behavior continued you would be alone, you would lose everything, and here you are. You are alone.

    You have lied to me and your siblings and friends, you have stolen thousands and thousands of dollars from me personally. Who knows what it all totals, with the countless times you helped yourself to my wallet. Stealing from Will with his ATM card. Stealing my credit card which I had to cancel on four different occasions. I sleep at night with my car keys, my phone (which you have stolen many times) and my wallet for fear of you. You deal drugs out of my home, which is not only illegal but also you are on probation. This is MY home and I am raising MY children.

*Imagine what Grace and Henry area dealing with, the embarrassment and shame that you have created in their lives. They are wonderful people scared and scarred by your behavior.*

*I have stood by your side in meetings at school, with the superintendent of schools because of your suspension, with the lawyers, which we hired three times for the three arrests. You lied to them, you have been lying to your probation officer. You failed at school, which we paid $40,000 for. You have burned bridges with teachers, coaches, friends, aunts, uncles, cousins, employers and your family.*

*And let's see. What did we give you, a beautiful home, a loving family, nice clothes, tons of food, boats, cars, vacations and an education. And you steal from me? You lie to me? We sent you to NOLS, and you left the program, we paid for it. You were asked to leave Insight Intensive, for stealing and bullying, we paid for it. I have hired psychologists, psychiatrists, anything for you, but I am as fucking crazy as you are for allowing this to continue.*

*You have made ZERO attempt to repay anything. You blame and justify all of your actions and behaviors. And as your swan song, you pawn my engagement ring, sell my Rolex watch, and God knows what else. You stole my laptop for drugs and blatantly lie that you did it. You stole from our neighbor and when he finds out he will press charges. You grabbed $4,000.00 from Dad's petty cash. Your behavior is monstrous.*

*You crashed my jeep and last week drove my car, popped the tire, cracked the wheel and a week later it is still in the shop because the alignment has been affected.*

*I will tell you this right now, you can not steal my mental, physical and emotional health. Until you own your behavior and take responsibility for your actions, I will take no part in this any longer. No calls, no family week, nothing. If and when you change your behavior, I will be there to support you, not a minute before.*

*And, if you leave the program and do not follow the recom-*

*mendations, not only will you never step foot in this home again, I am having you arrested and you will go to jail where you belong.*

*I love you, which is why I am paying AGAIN as the FINAL ditch effort to save your life.*

*mom*

*Jack fly fishing on the NOLS trip*

# THIRTY DAY LIMIT

During the summer of 2012, following a disaster year at Endicott College, Will told me that he discovered Jack in my closet. He asked, "What are you doing in Mom's closet, digging around looking for money?" No, it was jewelry. I didn't have much, but what I had, he took. My engagement ring, which I didn't wear anymore, but still had sentimental value. I wanted to have it reset for Grace. Back in my working days, I was an executive at both Polo Ralph Lauren and Tommy Hilfiger for a combined twenty three years. Tommy gave me a Rolex watch one Christmas. Grace had her eye on that, I didn't wear it. Now it was gone.

I preferred the Tag Heuer my dad gave me, anyway. He wore the same. I loved that watch. I gave the same style to Henry for his eighteenth birthday. He loved it. When Jack turned twenty, I gave him one, too. Henry said, "Why did you give him that watch?" Henry worked so hard at his stuff, school, friendships, all responsibilities. I knew he felt Jack didn't deserve it, and he didn't. I gave it to him because I didn't want to keep treating him like he was less. Big mistake, that was gone too.

Everything was gone, lap tops, motor scooters, skateboards. Apparently, some guy was giving Jack money to gather electronics and then sending the computers and other stuff to his home country. Will was on the case, finding out who he was, and where our stuff was.

Kevin was down in Norwalk at the pawn shop asking about my ring and watch. They were sold. Not sure about the watch, but he sold my ring for two hundred dollars. It had to be worth at least ten thousand dollars. Gone.

We intended Jack to go to NOLS, National Outdoor Leadership School, somewhere in Utah or Montana, I can't remember. Now, with the pawning incident it was NOLS or calling the police. I felt so violated, like he had no regard for me.

My friend and I were on a walk one day. We were talking about reincarnation and past lives. Since I started taking yoga classes, I'd been getting curious about spirituality, karma, the soul... I said to her, "I wonder what I was in my past life?" She replied, "A doormat?" Maybe. The people I love the most lie to me, cheat on me, and steal from me. Just walk all over me, yup, I was a doormat. Kevin even gave me a holiday doormat one Christmas! Cream background with red reindeer. It was cute, but didn't cover up the fact that it was a doormat.

Will and I called Dr. Caryn, the local psychologist who had been working with our family through all the stages of crazy. We had her on speaker telling her about Jack's most recent theft. I asked if I should call the police. She said that it was the drugs. Jack needed to be out of here, not in jail. We proceeded with the plan. It was all so foggy. My every day was filled with chaos and fear. He barely got on the trip because his physical didn't go so well—he had dirty urine. Obviously!

But he made it. He packed up and was ready for a three-month trek. What about all my things? I guess it didn't matter, as long as Jack was safe. We would deal with it on his return with a clear head, drug free and after time to reflect on his behavior. Sleeping outside, depending on teammates, learning survival (he already had that down pat), respecting the group and the land. Will said it would be better than rehab, sitting around with a bunch of addicts. We decided being out in the clean, fresh air, learning skills and developing friendships would be a better path for Jack.

I told him when he left that he needed to work hard on this trip to see the damage he had caused with his family relationships and friends. All of the lying, stealing, and drug use had changed him. I understood that his addiction caused him to act that way, but I was still furious with him. I communicated to him that he would need to earn our respect back.

And then he left. He was safe, out of this crazy place, now we could all try to put the pieces back together.

Thirty days in, he twisted his knee. Jack could always do thirty days, whether in rehab or on a trip like this, but not much more. He would get agitated and aggressive. He had injured his knee months earlier. He tore his ACL doing a back flip off a wake board on spring break, but the doctor said he was fit to go. Now, all of a sudden, the knee was a problem? The rescue squad had to go into the wilderness to get him and bring him back to base camp. He couldn't go back out. I knew it was bullshit, he had reached his thirty-day limit.

I said, "Jack, you need to complete three months, you can't come home until you do." I started my research. Colorado was a midway point home, so I started looking there. Insight Intensive was recommended.

This place was a restored camping facility. The kids grew their own organic vegetables, and they participated in all the cooking, meal prep and cleaning. There were tons of activities, kayaking, hiking trips, movie nights in town, workouts at the Denver Broncos training room. The accommodations were beautiful. Jack didn't like it.

On a trip to the Broncos training facility, Jack found a phone in the locker room. It belonged to one of the staff members. Returning to camp, they gathered around and the leader said there was a phone missing. He said he would overlook it as long as the individual told the truth and apologized. No one fessed up. The phone began to ring, in Jack's pocket.

That summer there was a severe drought in Colorado. The kids were advised where they could and could not smoke to prevent fire. Jack didn't follow the rules, and smoked where he was not supposed to. That and other repeated infractions led to the unthinkable—they kicked him out.

Jack was on a plane back home. I said he couldn't stay with us. We had normalcy in the house. Henry and Grace were just beginning a new school year, it was calm and orderly, and it needed to stay that way. He could stay with his dad.

Jack was to find work, which he did. Everyone would always show up and do what they could for Jack. Despite all the crazy, he was loved so much by his family, friends and neighbors. He got a job at the boatyard storing the boats for winter. The yard was close by, and he would be working for his friend's dad.

After some time, Jack said he wasn't getting along with Kevin and wanted to come home. Jack was disrespectful, calling Kevin out, and it would escalate to yelling. Jack always had his ear to the ground. He would overhear conversations, ask questions, find out the real story by putting two and two together. It didn't make for good in-house relations. I agreed to let Jack back under my roof. I wrote up my list of responsibilities and what I expected from him, and he had to agree to everything, then signed it. Despite his signature on my contract, the bad behavior continued. There was no remorse, no apparent second guessing any of it. I thought by now he would be learning from his mistakes, but he didn't seem to have any moral compass to detect right from wrong. It wasn't the first time I had done the "rules" sheet. I thought it would be different this time. I always had so much hope for him to overcome this troubled time of his life. After all he was eighteen, a teenager.

*June 6, 2012*

*Jack,*

    *I have written countless letters, we have had hundreds of conversations and here we are in the same situation. You are supposed to learn from your mistakes, but you don't seem to have any moral compass that detects right from wrong.*

    *This has been going on for years and I, for one, along with Dad and your entire family and extended family, are tired of it. Not even tired, over it! Your remorse lasts up to 12 hours, then the whole thing starts again. You need help. Lying and stealing are scum qualities and I am embarrassed for you.*

    *Your choices continue to lead you down paths that will have tragic results in your life and in your relationships. It has already begun and will continue to get worse.*

    *The ONLY way to a better life takes discipline, true honesty and hard work, which you have not demonstrated, not at home, at work, or at school.*

    *If you have stopped the pills that is a start, but you have caused serious trust issues with me and now Dad and your siblings.*

    *This is the deal Jack:*
- *You need to be in a program and see Caryn weekly*
- *You need to be on the job first thing tomorrow morning*
- *You need to be drug tested weekly*
- *You need to exercise daily*
- *You must treat your parents with the utmost respect*
- *You must follow the rules Dad puts forth for his home and boat*
- *You must pay me back $200.00 per week*
- *You must take the online class. Without effort in this area, school will not be an option for you at all.*

If these musts are not followed beginning right now, this means you cannot do this on your own and will be admitted to another program no later then July 1. If you don't choose to do that, then you are on your own.

The change MUST be dramatic. 180 degrees.

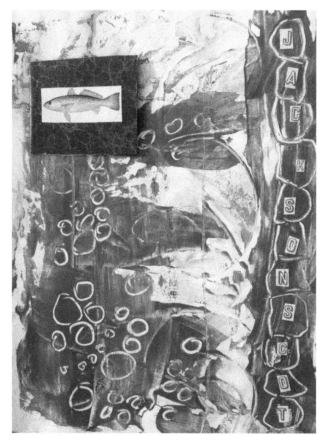

*Art Journal page, Fish*

Jack made an attempt at following the rules at home. Returning to school that fall was out. He needed to stay clean and be in a safe environment. He could worry about school in the spring.

We got through the holidays okay, but in February things started to go down hill. It started up again, him showing up late, leaving during a shift at work. There was a sense that something wasn't right. He was asked to leave the job, but was quickly hired close to home at another club, where he began doing the same thing. He would call and ask me to bring lunch, or he would make sandwiches to take to the job. Jack loved sandwiches. I never bought cold cuts unless he was home. He loved pickles, too. He was outdoors, working hard, but he couldn't stop. The pills, I assumed. He crushed them and snorted them for better effect. Smoking pot, cigarettes and pills. Not drinking so much, it wasn't his thing.

Once again, I began my research, and this time it needed to be rehab.

The pills had him, he couldn't fight it. I started to notice when he was high, his personality changed, his eyes would roll back in his head, and he would drool. It scared me.

I found Caron Pennsylvania, a highly recommended rehabilitation facility in the middle of rural Pennsylvania. He agreed to go, but when it was time and the two men in the van came to pick him up, he went crazy. Smoking weed until it was coming out his ears, wanting a last hit and a fix of pills. Kevin and my brother-in-law and the men got him in the van. He left.

Of course, the resident staff check through everything to make sure you are not bringing any contraband into the facility. Not just drugs, no phones, no books. This was rehab—we/he was in crisis. Now this is not shocking to me, but to them it was. Jack had his luxurious hair in a man bun and had stashed pills inside. They found them. But the better one was that he had his phone tucked up into his butt. Now the big butt was coming in handy. They asked him to do squats and it didn't fall out, even then. It wasn't until a week later they caught him listening to music on his phone and took it.

Pennsylvania in the middle of February and March was awful. Tons of snow. Jack never dressed warm. Jacket open and no gloves, he just pulled his hands up into his sleeves.

The Caron rehab program was designed with thirty days in Pennsylvania then a transfer to their other location in Boca Raton, Florida for the second portion of the program. Jack stayed in Pennsylvania for forty five days before he was ready for his transfer. The situation there was an apartment setting, where they had an allowance, had to buy and prepare their food, report to their group meetings and attend AA (Alcoholics Anonymous). He was clean, and doing a good job. Kevin and I had regular conference calls with his advisor, so as parents, we were delivering a consistent message. Jack was a wise ass to this guy, and they didn't seem to get along.

There would be consequences for not keeping the apartment clean, and for failing to attend a meeting or getting a sponsor. But he was clean and working the program. That was progress. We were able to speak with him; and he seemed happy.

On one grocery trip, a couple of the kids, including Jack, bought cough syrup and drank it all. They lied about it and had to leave the program and find their way. They were supposed to go to a meeting and find someone in recovery to take them in. After two days, they could petition to get back in. The two hosts could not be the same.

The first night Jack found someone to stay with, but the second night he couldn't or didn't want to. He hopped a fence at a nearby school and slept in a baseball dugout. He went back to his advisor and petitioned to get back in. He did, until they found out he lied about where he stayed the second night. That's when I got the call.

This time it so happened I was already in Florida. Grace, her new Irish sport horse, Herlique (her barn name is Heidi), and I were attending the Wellington Horse Show outside of Palm Beach. Grace had advanced her riding career to the children's jumpers. Sitting ringside with a cup of coffee chatting with a friend while Grace either lessoned or showed in the hunters was a pleasure for me, being a former equestrian myself. But the jumpers! That was terrifying, like I needed more fear in my life. The judging wasn't on how she or her animal presented themselves, it was clear the rails against the clock. High and fast, anyway you got over the fence was ok with the judge.

I received a call from Jack's advisor asking me to come to a group meeting at Caron Florida and confront Jack. I told the advisor that I had done everything. There was nothing I could do if Jack didn't follow the rules and didn't want to stay clean. I explained to Grace what was going on. I told her, "I've done everything." She replied, "You haven't done that." I changed my clothes and drove to Boca.

Jack was a little surprised to see me to say the least. I entered the meeting room, where the mixed group of males and females sat in a familiar circle. I have been to these meetings before. The leader of the group was there; he was who had phoned me. He called Jack out on his behavior in front of the group, then I let him have it too, in front of all of his peers. I was at my wits' end, emotionally and financially. Each one of these trips away cost fifty thousand dollars.

He kind of giggled like a school child while I was in there. I think he was embarrassed. When the group meeting concluded, I went up to Jack and gave him a big hug.

"I love you, please please behave."

"I will Mom! I love you too."

As we walked out together, he asked for money for cigarettes. I didn't give it to him. He had an allowance that was all accounted for to keep the kids on the straight and narrow.

Jack continued with the program and started the working portion. He found a job answering phones a few miles away. He got a bike somehow and rode there every day for his work. Following his day's work, he had to attend "group" and an AA meeting. He would FaceTime me and Grace. He was in a cubicle. You couldn't put Jack in a box.

He developed friends and even a girlfriend. He knew that was not allowed if you were following twelve steps, especially so early on. He needed to focus on himself and his sobriety, not a girlfriend. She was in the program too, an alcoholic. This was not her first rodeo.

This portion of the Caron program was about six weeks. A court date was on the calendar back in Connecticut, and he was going to have to appear. This was never good. Home held lots of triggers for Jack. He came home around the end of the summer. Once again, he stayed with his dad. He didn't follow my rules the last time, and it wasn't going to happen to me, Henry and Grace again.

Jack did some odd jobs at home with his dad and went to a couple of meetings. I do know that he wanted to get back to Florida, to his girlfriend and his job. Court was taking longer than we thought, as it always did. I told Jack I would fly his girlfriend up for a weekend since he was doing such a good job. They had fun on the water, boating, fishing and doing all things Jack. She didn't stay long because she said she thought he was lying to her about using. He wasn't around the house that much so I didn't notice it.

This cycle was now becoming a pattern. Come home, legal stuff, pick up, end in rehab. As the cycle continued, it began to escalate. I remember one Thanksgiving at my parents' farm. We were all there, lots of fun, as always, but it wasn't the same anymore. My dad had always been at the center of singing, baking and joking, he was now gone. Kevin always loved Thanksgiving at the farm, laughing, singing, running around with the kids, but now he was gone too. I could tell Jack was getting agitated. "Mom? When are we leaving?" He would follow me around, staring at me until I agreed it was time to go.

Christmas was sketchy. The rest of the family were all around the dining room table, singing our plumb pudding song. Where was Jack? He probably slipped out the back, I wasn't sure, but he was gone.

Still at home, still on probation, still on drugs, the winter continued. Jack stayed at Kevin's, but he would come home for dinner and to snuggle with Grace. Kevin and Jack seemed to be getting along much better. Thank God!. Henry was now in college in Boston, and Will had made Nashville his home. So, it was just us girls and Jack.

I was driving home from a boxing workout with my trainer and speaking to Will on the phone. Down the road, I saw a figure walking, well, wobbling, headed toward my house. "Will, I have to call you back." It was Jack. I stopped the car. He was messed up, he needed me.

Sherry, my yoga teacher and dear friend on Martha's Vineyard, would sometimes tell us about the Hindu gods and goddesses in class. One of my favorites was Kali. In downward facing dog, body burning, her voice would come to our ears, talking about this badass goddess who represented fierce maternal love. Often depicted as black or dark blue, holding the head of a demon in one hand and a knife in the other, slicing its head off and drinking the blood. Yep, that was supposed to represent love. Seems odd, but it is love. "Like the strength gathered when a mom lifts a car off her child," Sherry would say. That "don't fuck with me, or my kids" love.

With Kali energy, I lifted Jack into the front seat. That's what it had to be. Jack was two hundred and twenty pounds, and I lifted him into the car. He was so messed up, so heavy. He couldn't walk. I knew it was bad. Distraught, I drove him home.

I had him lie down while I researched detox places. I knew he was in trouble, but I didn't have the resources. I called New Haven, Danbury, nothing was working. I got him in the car and took him to the nearby Norwalk Hospital Emergency Room. When we got there, Jack refused to go inside. The security guard at the door couldn't do anything to help me. Jack didn't want to go in. He paced around my car, still wobbling. I just needed to get him inside. "Please, Jack! Get in the door!"

Finally, when we got in, he was placed in the hall on a gurney. It was too crowded for a room. I didn't know what he was on, I assumed pills. I never did find out. I stayed for a while. They said they couldn't send him anywhere until he completed a psych evaluation. He was too out of it to do it. He was too out of it to do anything. I stood outside the bathroom while he repeatedly dropped the urine cup. Over and over again. I don't think they ever tested him. In retrospect, I think it must have been heroin.

Jack was getting agitated and defiant on the gurney. He kept pushing me to let him leave the hospital. I knew he should stay. It was difficult for me to be there with him when he was like that. I quietly left, telling the attendants it would be better for him and me if I wasn't there. They said they would keep him for twenty four hours. He was in good hands.

I went home and poured a stiff drink. Then the phone rang, the fucking phone. It was Kevin, who had gone to see Jack in the Emergency Room.

"Jack's not here, they let him leave."

Oh my God. He must have called one of his friends to come get him. I called his cell and he picked up. I told him he must come home immediately, which he did. I put him to bed and I slept on the floor at the bottom of his stairs so he wouldn't leave.

The next day, it was back to the phone again. No rehab facility would take him without going to detox first. Now to find detox.

I found one in Danbury that had one spot left but he had to do an intake over the phone. He managed to do it. We'd gotten the ball rolling. He told me he was getting agitated again and wanted to get some weed to calm him down. I agreed. First we went to Kevin's to gather clothes. I waited in the car. After too long, I went in after him. I walked in on him wobbling around with a belt in his hand. Oh my God, he was shooting up. I grabbed his clothes, put him in the car, and drove to get the weed so he wouldn't freak out. The kid gave me a bud. I gave him the money and screeched away.

It was a forty-minute drive to Danbury. The entire way there Jack was trying to roll a joint on his lap. His eyes were rolling back in his head. It would seem like he was sleeping, then his head would go off to the side and come back up. He told me he liked being in the space where nothing mattered, he was free there. Who am I, where am I, what am I doing? I am Barbara, in my car, driving seventy miles an hour up Route Seven to get my son to detox. To save my son's life.

I pulled up to the iron gate and it opened. I drove in, and the nurses came to greet us. I told them Jack was in the car smoking. Opening the door, she said, "Come on Jack, let's go in side." She had it, she had seen this before. Like the bad puppy, he followed. I gave him a hug, and he was gone.

What I didn't know until two days later was that while he was filling out his paper work, he went down. They called an ambulance, but were already prepared with a narcan injection. Narcan reverses opioid overdose. It was relatively new then, but now most all first responders carry it. Nearly dead, he had overdosed. I was minutes away from this happening on my watch, with no resources. I saw the timing as divine intervention. After two days in detox, he was ready to be picked up and transported to High Watch Rehabilitation Facility. Now this was no frills, Twelve Steps, no amenities, just working the program. We wanted to get it right.

Those successful in recovery regularly attend meetings, find a sponsor for support, and work the steps. The first step was admitting you were powerless over alcohol, pills, whatever the addiction was, and that your life was unmanageable. Step two, acknowledge that there was a power greater than yourself that can restore sanity. Step three, make a decision to turn your will and life over to the care of God, as you understand him. Step four, make a searching and fearless moral inventory of yourself. This was the step, Jack told me, that he kept getting stuck on. He could not seem to go deep into himself, and then he would pick up.

He was there for thirty days. Grace and I would visit. He looked great, was working out. Jack was back!

He asked to stay for another two weeks, said he wanted success. So happy. He worked with an exit coordinator on staff to plan next steps. They agreed Sober Living was the only option. Jack chose a place called By The Sea Recovery in San Diego, a lovely spot, with in-house management, AA meetings, a plan to write resumes, volunteer, look for work or go back to school. It was a good plan, a fresh start, away from here. He was excited. He was going to Cali!

Ideally, he should have gone from High Watch directly to the airport, but two things happened. One, he had a court date that he needed to attend before he left, and two, he got kicked out of the facility a few days early. I couldn't believe it, this time it was for fraternizing with the girls. It was not allowed, there were rules. Jack thought they didn't apply to him. I had to go pick him up.

It wasn't but a day until the whole cycle started again. I called my friend Jen. Jen was very connected in the sober community. She is an amazing woman, a warrior, loving mom and friend. She inspired me and Jack as she faced her own struggles. Jen helped me to understand the root of addiction and the life-long battle Jack faced. She knew that addiction was a disease and should be treated as such, that success could be reached by attending regular meetings, surrounding yourself with friends in recovery, and getting a sponsor. Following the Twelve Steps was a life-long commitment.

She invited me, when Jack was struggling, to a prayer breakfast in Norwalk. The speaker was a man named Gary Mendell. He began the organization Shatterproof after his son tragically died after being clean for a year. I listened and ate breakfast, but didn't grasp that this was where Jack was headed. I should have been more attentive.

Jen hooked me up with a sober companion right away for Jack. I hired this old hippie, at fifteen hundred dollars per day, to stay with Jack until his court date. Then it would be off to the airport. I don't know how he did it, where he got it. He had no money, no car, a sober companion, but he still picked up drugs.

When the court date was complete, I drove him to the airport. I could tell he was on something, and I was afraid he was going to open the door while I was driving over the Whitestone Bridge and jump. I got him to check in to his flight, and I gave him a big hug, "I love you Jack." I think I almost had a heart attack, again.

It was arranged that someone from By The Sea would pick him up at the airport, which they did. First things first, a urine test. He tested dirty, and therefore they wouldn't take him. Had to go to detox.

I did not know what to do. He couldn't stop, or he didn't want to. He said he liked to be in that place of nothingness. I don't know.

The people in San Diego detox were great, and like most people they took a special liking to Jack. The woman at the detox had a friend who ran a sober house, and arranged to have him pick up Jack. This place and set up was nothing like what we had arranged. It was far from most things, and he didn't have a car. Getting a job was tough, but he seemed to be ok. He liked being in Cali, but he wanted to be by the water.

Jack seemed to be working the program and making new friends, one in particular was Emily. Jack loved the girls, but he was supposed to be focusing on himself, not the needs of others. We talked and texted and all was well. I told him if things were still going well, I would come to San Diego for his twenty first birthday on September 2, 2014, which I did,.

I got a room at a nice hotel in Del Mar and rented a car. I drove up and met Jack and Emily for the day. He looked great, and she was lovely. They seemed to really like each other. We ate and swam and had birthday cupcakes and gifts. It was going to be a short stay, but it was important for us to have this time together. "I love you, Jack."

Then something sketchy happened. Emily, Jack and I were working on his resume in the hotel office. Emily was at the keyboard. He could do so many things and worked at many places, so the resume was looking strong. Emily had to go, so Jack walked her out. Minutes passed, I waited. They were gone a really long time. Finally, after too long, I walked out the front, and saw Jack taking my car from the valet. Are you kidding me?

"I'm in there working on your resume, and you are taking my car. Where are you going?"

"Emily, forgot her phone," he said. This mumbo jumbo of lies rolled off his tongue.

"Well, I'll drive with you."

I can't believe I was so stupid not to have just called his phone, because he was holding his, not Emily's, and lying to me. We pulled out, down the street and back to the hotel. I decided to leave then. I did not feel safe.

I never told anybody that. I know with addiction, relapse is a part of it. But this was insane. He never got the getaway car. Where was he going?

*October 8, 2012*

*Jack,*

*I can't believe I am going to write another letter. They have not worked before, so I don't know why I think it might work now. We have been at this for so long. I took Grace to the ER this morning (her earring went into her ear and had to be removed), but I was reminded of you lying on the bed after putting your hand through the window. I was so terrified at the direction of your life then and I still am. Truth be known, if you didn't have that injury, we were sending you to the Adirondacks for a mountain program. Your bag was packed. The turn of events left you at home and I was so relieved because I didn't want you to go, even though it was best for you.*

*I thought this summer was going to be ok, you promised to work, exercise, pay back debt and get your life in order, but that didn't work. Then I thought it was going to be NOLS, then renaissance and back to school for fall, starting out fresh. That didn't work. Then I thought you would complete the program, dig down deep and work, exercise, pay the debt, be responsible for your life in a healthy way, and now I see that is not working either.*

*I really don't know when or if you will turn your life around. I do know that it is so painful to watch. I did think (as did Henry and Grace) that there were signs of improvement. I think what happens is you think you have it, then start to ease up on the discipline because you feel better and then one by one things start slipping backwards.*

*I am so familiar with this. I remember Dad coming back from rehab, for depression, looking and feeling good. Up exercising, reading his meditations, going to work, coming home for dinner. Then, sleeps in, skips breakfast, the book is left unopened, exercise stops, works through dinner and then back in bed for days.*

*If I could fix this for you, I would, but I have tried everything. I know you said I didn't want to have any part of you, but the truth is, I cannot be part of your demise. I think Will said the same thing to you, we love you too much.*

*Your program is over in a month. This final stretch is up to you. You can work at this every day, which means getting up with the rest of the world at 8, exercising, eating right, managing your personal hygiene, gong to work and going to school and programs. Every day! Coming up with a plan and commitment for your immediate future, or get a full time job, since you will be finished with the programs, find yourself a room/apartment and get on with your life. You are over staying your welcome over at Henson's and it is time to move on.*

*Henry and Grace are working hard at school, taking SAT's, applying to colleges. We live a "normal life," no chaos and crazy behavior, and we are not going back to that. They have their own responsibilities and relationships that will be protected in this safe environment. There are no pills, paraphernalia, small baggies, cigar tobacco and etc. I do not have to look over my shoulder to see if anyone is taking my money or credit cards, reading my emails, taking my things. I feel safe, although I still lock up my wallet and sleep with my keys.*

*The fact that you just take (steal) and treat yourself to hundreds of dollars of clothing, and feel no guilt, or nod from your conscience that it is wrong, is beyond worrisome. It is really a severe problem that goes beyond drug use. It is the inability to live within social norms.Healthy mined people would not do this, and you do it repeatedly.*

*If you are considering moving back here and going to school, you better get yourself out of bed and moving forward. You must come up with a plan, we are not paying for school for you to stay in your room, it is throwing money away.*

*We are already making plans for Thanksgiving at the farm then to Princeton with the Kings for the weekend. I have the Megrue's place in Stratton for Christmas week and dinner at home. Plans are underway for spring breaks, Florida horse show, Henry heli-skiing in Canada, Turks and Caicos and more. I/we hope that you will be a part of this family, in a happy and healthy way.*

I heard the other night that we cant change.. We were put on this earth the way we were meant to be. But by proceeding to fill my body with things it doesn't need im altering my path in life. To a point where i sit and think what if i cant get this right? what if this dark place im in is where ill be for the rest of my existance. I hear people say it gets better, but right now that seems hard to imagine. The world is moving around me, people doing things in their lives, going places happy.. I dont get why i cant seem to move on with my life. my girlfriend cheated on me, which makes me feel worthless, and inadiquet. Im here for a reason i just need to find out what

It is exactly I was put on this earth to do. I would like to be closer to "GOD" whatever that is for me because I cant do this on my own.

I keep trying to make sense in what has happened and is continuing to happen but maybe Im not supposed to know the next step. All I can worry about is NOW! or ill get all fucked up. I feel like ive ~~always~~ had experiences with "god moments" just things people say and things I see throughout my day.(The book of Eli)?! about FAITH → you walk this path blind, but with faith that god will get you where you need to be. "Let Go Let God" always thought of it to be a gay quote, but

Its the truth! I need to be
guided in my life by someone who
knows what it is I'm here for.
Mikes death still has me in
shock. Its so crazy how someone
is here one day and gone the next.
**WHY** am I still here. What is
so important about my being that
others that havent put their life
in danger like I have arent here
any more. I'm not sure whats
going to happen to me but I guess
its not up to me.
I always feel so Alone... Its something
I havent been able to shake for
sometime now and I dont know
if I ever will. I have no INNER
HAPPINESS and I think that is what
prevents me from being at peace with
myself.

I'm always ~~the~~ surrounded by chaos, but created by me. My whole world has fallen apart around me ALONE and I dont know where to turn... To just give up know or dig my self out of this dark hole I'm in

" Nothing others do is because of you. what others say and do is a projection of their own reality, their own dream. When you are IMMUNE to the opinions and actions of others you wont be the victim of needless suffering –"

*Jack's journal entry, not dated, written in California,*
*in a leather bound journal I gave him.*

*November 4, 1993*

*Dearest Snuggle baby Jack,*

*It has been a busy month, you are so alert, kicking and smiling. Noticing Mommy and Daddy and Willie. Willie has been a bit rough with you. An occasional tug or nibble.*

*Mommy had to go back to work but started working two days at home so I could snuggle you. Also so I could attend a bible study on Wednesdays at church. Your baptism was on Oct. 31. It was lovely. Performed by my new pastor friend, of course. We reaffirmed our love for Jesus and confessed our commitment to raise you in a Christian home, living by the word of God. I will do my best.*

*She prayed for you and Willie and Harry. It was very special. Afterward we had our family brunch. More gifts - you are a very special baby.*

*It was also Halloween. Willie and Cam were knights. Daddy went trick or treating. He was an Indian. You and mommy were baseball players handing out candy.*

*I'm on a diet - boy am I hungry! Daddy is sleeping in the chair. Willie has gone to bed and you are sleeping next to me in the white basket, snoring a tiny bit. Sleep tight little baby. May God watch over you this night, I'll see you in the morning light.*

*Love,*
*Mommy xo*

*Thanksgiving at the farm, all the cousins, November 2013*

# WHOLEHEARTED

Once upon a time I was very involved in the church.

I went to the Presbyterian Church as a kid. Big, old, stone, cold church. I remember Sunday school and pancake breakfasts, running around, not really learning anything. Lots of old people. I liked church, I always did. My siblings and I were all baptized in the church and dressed up every year for Easter Sunday. Spring dresses in cold weather was what I remembered.

As a college student, I was feeling spiritually lost and I asked to go to the new Presbyterian Church my parents found near our New Jersey home. I had never been confirmed so I wasn't really committed and felt I needed some guidance.

Ends up, I loved the service, the message, the hymns, the light in the space. So different from the dark, seemingly wet stone church of my childhood. I asked to see the pastor, Harry Chase. He came to our home and I told him, as an adult, I would like to belong to the church. We all needed to belong to something. I wasn't sure what it would entail, but I was prepared to make the commitment. He asked if I believed in God. I said I did. And he said, "Well then, you are welcome to join."

The following Sunday during the service, I was asked to come forward to the front of the church. He put his hand on my head and welcomed me to the congregation.

Years later, he married me and Kevin. He was a lovely, faithful man.

Time went on, college, work, and everything else, and church wasn't on my radar so much. When I was working in New York, I did attend the Fifth Avenue Presbyterian Church for different series led by a wonderful pastor, until he was asked to leave following an affair with a parishioner. What is it about successful, powerful men? Hundreds of members hanging on the hope of God, Heaven, eternal life. Honor, commitment, family importance, even with his family standing by his side at the altar. Talking on and on about his wife and two boys, all the while having an affair with a church member. That's messed up. It seems to happen frequently with men in power, clergy, elected officials, successful businessmen.

Pregnant with my first baby, I felt it was important to raise my family with the influence of a wholesome church. Kevin was Catholic, but agreed to take the new members classes with me. We both became members of our new church. My babies were in that church from the crib room through confirmation. Every Sunday was Sunday school followed by trips to Donut Inn and family swap with cousins all over the place. My siblings, Leslie and Cathy, and I lived very close to each other and we were always pregnant at the same time. Most all of our children have a matching cousin.

Kevin and I taught Sunday school. We were very involved with the members, and the kids were involved in all the activities. Women's retreats, Christmas dinners with crafts, Shack (a barn behind the church for middle schoolers). My extended family was involved, too. My sister Leslie and her husband, Chris, were teachers as well. Chris was a deacon. Their first child Andrew, the oldest cousin, did not have a matching cousin. Cameron, next up, was the matching cousin to Will. Christian a match to Henry.

My sister Cathy and her husband, Steve, always sat in the third pew, same seat. Cathy was a brilliant chef, and she catered all the church events. Cathy's son Kenny's matching cousin was Harry, that did not last. Her other son, Robert, was Jack's match. Jack loved Robert and Kenny. Robert lived near Jack in San Diego. My brother, Rob, and his wife, Linda, were not as involved in the church, but occasionally came. Olivia was Grace's match while Cathryn doesn't have one. They wanted me to have another baby so Cathryn would have match, but that wasn't happening.

When Harry died, the first one to come to the emergency room was the new young associate pastor. The ambulance had come to take Harry away to the hospital. Kevin and I had followed behind in the car. The ambulance was driving so slow, I remember thinking they needed to drive faster. I was so afraid. We were sitting in the hospital waiting room, and we still had not heard what was happening with Harry. I noticed her when she walked in, her blond hair, fair skin, her clear blue eyes found me right away. As soon as she took the first step towards me, I knew. She introduced herself, lay a hand on my shoulder, and said the words that I feared the most. That was our first meeting. She told me Harry had died.

Oh my God, this can't be happening. I was so lost. They can't take my baby! No no NO. I just held my head, flooded with tears, this can't be true. No no NO.

They wanted me to say goodbye. What? He was just two months old. He was beautiful and strong, my sweet little baby boy. No, don't make me say goodbye. He was lying on the gurney with a sheet up to his neck. He was beautiful, so soft but pale, so peaceful. I didn't want to do it, but she encouraged me. I kissed him on the tummy and said goodbye to my new born little baby boy. I had to leave the hospital without him. Oh my God!

SIDS, they said, Sudden Infant Death Syndrome.

She came by our house every day. I waited at my window for her station wagon to pull up. She brought me a Bible and read passages to me. She told me more about God and Jesus than I knew before. I listened, hanging on every word. She said God knew the number of hairs on my head. She told me how much Jesus loved me, and that he was holding Harry. We would read scripture together. At night, I would lie in bed with my eyes closed and try to talk to Jesus and to see my baby. Nothing.

I dove into the church. I went on all the women's retreats. I spoke at different venues including the Pittsburgh Theological Seminary. I spoke on God's love for us and his Grace. I was asked to speak on Easter Sunday at my church and share my resurrection story. Easter Sunday at my own church, the same podium where I stood so many years later to celebrate Jack's life. I had come a long way and the church held me up the whole time.

One summer, we arranged a family vacation to Scotland, our homeland. This trip was with my sister Leslie and all the matching cousins. By this time, all the kids were bigger, no longer babies and toddlers, but no one was out of their teens. We rented an amazing farm house deep in a valley of hills that reached straight up from the backyard. The hills were filled with heather and echoing with the sounds of flocks of sheep. The trip started in London, then we took a train to Edinburgh, and ended the trip with my family heading to Costa Brava, Spain, another favorite spot.

When we arrived at the farm house, the kids immediately started running up the hills that went on forever. It reminded me of our family trips home to see my grandmothers and cousins when we were "wee." I organized everything, flights, trains, hotels, reservations, rental cars, but the owner said that they did not provide sheets for the beds. What? I didn't realize it wasn't customary. While Kevin and I climbed the hills to see the spectacular view, he said, "You didn't take care of the sheets?"

I did everything, every thing. They provided us the sheets, in the end. I couldn't make him happy.

On the trip, I asked Kevin if he would go to counseling with me. I felt our marriage was unstable and we needed help. He agreed he would when we returned home.

My first stop returning from our trip was in the office of my friend and pastor. She was a small group companion and Tres Dias group member. Tres Dias is a three-day global Christian movement to bring the participants closer on their personal walk with God. A small group of former Tres Dias attendees would gather weekly to support each other to stay on track. We were tight. She gave me the name of a Christian marriage counselor who was close to home. Leaving the church parking lot, I called him and got an appointment.

Kevin and I went in the early fall for our first session. We drove separately. His office was in his home on the water in Stamford. Nice enough. I explained I felt our communication was deteriorating with intimacy as its companion. He was a nice man, seemed to be. I did most of the talking; Kevin didn't say much. He told me that he needed to work with Kevin first and that I would join soon thereafter. That's weird, I thought, I understood that we would be going together.

Kevin kept at it and I kept out of it. Ends up, there were some relationship issues with someone other then me. I called the counselor's office. I was told I was to call again right away if he didn't pick up and he would know it was an emergency. This was an emergency. I confronted the counselor and my husband, as they were in session at the time. It was true.

More pain. Anger. Fear.

I went to my pastor. I told her what I had learned. She looked at me with those blue glass eyes that had a direct link to heaven. She said, "I know."

"Wait, what? You know? Why didn't you tell me?"

She said it was "professional courtesy." What the heck? You are my pastor, my friend, you've betrayed me. No, that's not okay. Not at all.

I did not go back to that church.

Years of wandering. No church, no real belief system, no faith. Empty.

I left church and found yoga during this time. Not that yoga is a religion, but it was a good way to fill the void, and a good path for me. I have now been practicing yoga for fifteen years. The yoga journey challenged and peeled away many of my old beliefs. It instilled curiosity in me and helped me grow. I did miss the community of church and the hymns, though. I loved to sing. Maybe it was time to rekindle my church fire after all these years.

My sister Cathy and I tried out a few new churches. We would meet up on Sundays. We tried our original church, and then tried the Calvary Baptist Church. We really liked the Baptist Church because we knew the pastor and felt very welcome there. Then we tried Talmadge Hill, a little community church in a neighboring town. Cathy's neighbor's mom had passed, and we went to the service there. It was just past New Years 2015, I'll never forget. The entire family were wearing New Year's Eve hats as they spoke of the love they had for their mom, mother-in-law, grandmother. When I walked in, I felt such warmth and sense of community. It was casual and comfortable. I knew this pastor also. These were my people, it felt like home. Years with no church and now I had found my place.

My sister always wants to sit in the front. I always sat in the balcony or at the back, but this church was small and had no balcony. Well, we sat in the front and I cried through the entire service, I mean sobbing. The next Sunday, the same thing. I had been wandering for so many years, and now I finally found a place of peace and comfort—and I could wear my snow boots. I liked it there, I was home.

We went every Sunday, and every Sunday I cried the entire service. On the way out one Sunday, Mitch the pastor said, while shaking my hand, "Would you like a pastoral visit?" Ya think? I'm a mess. My baby died, my marriage is over, my son is a drug addict, I'm afraid, and yes, I need a pastoral visit!

I arranged to see him very soon after. I went to his office and rambled on about my story. Everyone has one, you know. I felt however that mine deserved a chapter in the Bible, somewhere after Job. He didn't disagree. I told my new pastor I didn't feel like I had a religion, had gotten off the path, and I couldn't find my way back. He told me that I had perhaps outgrown religion, that my path was now one of spirituality. I had outgrown Heaven and Hell and the Bible stories, and now I had awakened to something even greater.

Mitch asked me to consider the possibility of wholeheartedness, a word coined by Brene Brown, a researcher, author and storyteller. The concept offers the ability to accept our lives and circumstances as a whole. Not dividing things into good or bad, but just accepting all of it as part of the package, a part of the whole. Wholeheartedness. Yes, it allowed life, existence, to be more than just good or bad, heaven or hell, promise or sin. It was both, and it was all of it. I liked it. It felt right.

When Jack was home, I brought him to my new church. He looked so handsome in his khakis and navy cashmere sweater. We had a laugh about something. That always happened at church. Of course we were in the front row because of my sister and there were probably only twenty, if that, in the congregation. I felt a tap on my shoulder. A member and friend whispered in my ear. "Is that your son? He is so handsome."

I was so happy Jack was with me. We would be living a wholehearted life.

*March 20, 2016*

*Jackamo,*

*I had a dream I had another baby. He was so big and you looked the same as him. I can't wait to have grandchildren. That is what this life is, slow and takes forever, but then it's not it goes so fast. One section after the other. Now I'm in an alone section. Jen calls it the hallway before another door opens. We'll see. I guess anything could happen. I will learn to talk to you myself and we can talk all the time without fear, lies or anger. Just love, right? That's all there is from what I have learned and we are all connected, all part of God, the source. Just little pieces of the whole. Makes sense I guess, there is nothing else that makes sense to me.*

*Grace and Jack dancing on his last visit home*

# WESTPORT COUCH

This visit home for Jack was the final final. He had to clear up his biggest outstanding legal issue, which was selling pills. Kevin was very helpful with all the legal stuff, as he was good at navigating the system. It all scared me. The charge was from the time he was arrested face down in the middle of town on the same day I exchanged the Porsche for my big black truck. That day. But this was it. He needed to go to court and convince the prosecution that he should be admitted into this outpatient rehabilitation program, for which the defendant must be so much of a drug addict that he sold the drugs to support his habit and not for profit. Jack came back home to do the convincing. It was in February, following our Christmas in Cali. What an awful time to come back east, to the cold, damp and gray.

I was afraid for Jack to return, it always went south. And it did quickly. Jack came home, and it was just the three of us, me, Jack and Grace. Jack and Grace were in love. They sat together in the same chair watching TV and played this annoying game where they finished each other's sentences at the same exact time. That made me nuts. Jack looked great, he was standing tall, in good shape. I always told him when he came home it was like putting Humpty Dumpty together again. Hair cut, dentist, new sneakers, athletic clothes. This time we added getting his passport application in. We drove around together, me in the passenger seat and Jack at the wheel. He was a great driver. I wasn't going to let him out of my sight.

It was four in the morning. I rolled over and saw the light shining around my bedroom door. That was how I always knew when Jack was home and in bed, the light would go out. I listened, but never could hear his footsteps, so the light was my indicator. He didn't actually have a room, it was a loft. I got out of bed and climbed his stairs to check on him.

His bathroom light was on. As I got closer, I could see his legs coming out of the bathroom into his room. He was lying on the floor. A needle to his side. I shook him and shook him, his eyes opened, dazed. I was screaming, "Jack, get up, wake up!" He sat up. As I fell to the floor, I heard the guttural wailing I remembered from Harry's death. It was a frightening noise. It was coming from me. He came to my side, and said, "Mom, I'm ok. Breathe." He asked me if I wanted Klonopin? I was so afraid, shaking, I couldn't catch my breath through my sobs. He started packing up his things.

Grace was asleep; it was a school night. When it became light, I called Kevin and asked him to come and get Jack. I called my sisters Leslie and Cathy. They were there in minutes. Just like when I found Harry. I called 911, then Leslie, she arrived first.

Kevin came and took Jack. I told Grace what happened. She asked if he had a needle, and I told her the truth.

I immediately got online to try to find a sober house. Jack could not be here without supervision, and mine was not enough. In California, there was a sober house on every corner. It really wasn't a "thing" here in Connecticut, but I found one in the neighboring town of Westport called The Westport House. They had one opening and he was in.

Jack was detoxing again. They offered him Suboxone, a drug used to minimize withdrawal symptoms. He refused. He told the house manager he wanted to feel this terrible withdrawal, the pain and nausea, so he would remember how bad it was to help prevent him from using again. It took days, and he was safe and in good care. There were a bunch of young guys in the house, there mostly for the excessive use of weed. Jack called them "newbies," beginners. They had activities, worked out, ate well, and went to meetings.

There were five weeks from the original court date to the final one. That was too long, but there was nothing we could do. He needed to be safe and wait it out. Once he was settled in, I opened up the door I had closed so many times, testing the waters with Jack. I went up to the house, met the managers, and spent some time watching movies with the guys. It was so cold and snowy out, they spent a lot of time indoors. They called it the Westport Couch instead of Westport House because they were on the couch watching TV so much.

Jack was feeling better, and working on his health. He told me if this happened to him again he was going to die. It took him out so quickly, he said. To which I replied, "Then stop doing it!"

During his stay at the Westport Couch, following the morning routine of meetings, exercise and breakfast, I would pick up Jack. We ran errands together. I would make stuff up just to keep us busy. We usually ended up at the same restaurant for a late lunch. We were so regular we just walked in and took the same table each time, bypassing the hostess. We would call Grace and she would meet us after school. We always got the mussels.

Jack's teeth were an outstanding issue. They had terrible decay due to the pill use. It took time to get them back in shape. Our dentist was aware of his problem, she could tell by his mouth. The bigger problem at the moment was he had to get his wisdom teeth out. The back teeth were growing in sideways and they would eventually impact.

We had the time and opted to get them out during this visit. And so he did—with no anesthesia. Just Tylenol. He was in terrible pain for days. I nursed him back by heading to Westport with smoothies and other icy options. His head was wrapped with ice and he was propped up on the good old Westport Couch.

Weeks went by, and it was time for court. I took a great screenshot from my computer with Jack standing behind me in a nice suit, so handsome, off to his court date. It was a Thursday, then one more night in Westport, and then, hopefully, if he gets into the program, back to Cali. So close.

The court date went well. He made it! He was deemed so much of a drug addict that he got into the program. I guess we should have been happy about this? The felony charge for dealing was dropped.

A clean slate—Jack had been clean for more than thirty days, his legal record was clean, his wisdom teeth were out, passport ordered, he made it. Phew. My mind was already moving ahead. I could keep on schedule with Grace and head to Florida for her horse show Friday after school. Jack had one more day at Westport House and a ticket home for Saturday morning. I said goodbye to him on Thursday with "I love you Jack."

Grace and I arrived around five in the afternoon. We had a buttoned-up routine of flying to West Palm, picking up our rental, and heading into town for dinner at the same Italian restaurant, Bice. We always ordered the same thing. Grace would get the pappardelle noodles with tomato basil sauce and the mozzarella melted in. I would have a Grey Goose martini, straight up with olives, and the fish of the day. We'd split the salad. From there we would drive to Wellington to the show.

While we were driving, Grace was on her phone, of course. She said to me, "Mom, Christian is doing really well." He had been involved along with Jack in dangerous behavior for a while.

"Oh really, why do you say that?"

"He just texted me, wishing me luck at the show. He says he and Jack are at the house in the Jacuzzi."

What? Why was Jack at the house? How did he get there? Christian doesn't drive. Why wasn't he at Westport House? They were supposed to take him to the airport the next day.

I called Jack. Grace said, "Mom don't, they'll know it was me who told." I absolutely did not care about that. I had that feeling, it was back, something wasn't right, I felt it in my gut. I always told Grace if it doesn't feel right, it's not.

"Jack, what are you doing at the house?" He convinced Kevin to let him stay at his house for the last night, and he was at my house doing his laundry. He said he was going to drive Christian home, and have dinner and sleep at Dad's. No, this was not ok.

"How do you have a car?"

"I drove my friend Katie to the train. She said I could use it while she was in New York." Jack was so resourceful. No! He couldn't have money, he couldn't have a car, and he needed to be supervised.

Christian lived by the Stamford border, and I knew Jack had dealers there. I called Kevin. I told him to get to the house, he had to drive Christian home, and bring Jack back to his place." I don't know why you have strayed from the plan, it was supposed to be Westport House to the airport." I know how it happened. Jack could be so convincing and manipulative. Kevin just wanted to be with him one last night.

Kevin never went to the house. Jack drove Christian home and went to his dad's.

Later we found the text to the dealer. He said he had three minutes to get whatever he was getting and then he had to get to his dad's. I knew it.

Henry said, "They never could put Humpty together again."

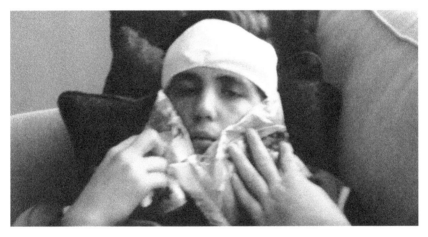

*Jack at Westport House following wisdom teeth extraction, February 2015*

*May 14, 1994*

*My sweet baby Jack. I love you so! My arms feel empty without you but I know you are in Gods care and I have nothing to fear.*

*You are becoming such a big boy. Two teeth below, lots of crawling. Popping everything in your mouth. You chuckle and giggle at Willie. You really think he is something special, and he is.*

*You love the water, especially your bathtub. Daddy took you in the pool when we went to Florida for Granny's surprise 60th birthday. You were eating lots of shells on the beach. You are so snuggly. We will be moving soon and you will be in your new house and nursery. I want it to be so nice for you.*

*Daddy, Willie and I love you so much !*

*Trust in the Lord with all your Heart.*

*Lo, I am with you always. The Lord is with you Jack and with your angel brother.*

*I love and adore you,*

*Mommy xo*

# SAN FRANCISCO?

Some kind of crazy was going on Saturday before the airport. I didn't understand. Kevin and Jack somehow missed two flights. Chaos was emerging, I could feel it throughout my body, through the phone and text lines all the way to Florida. But Jack got on the plane and he was off. Jack can be explosive and when drugs are looming in the background, it gets scary.

Grace and I made it home, back to school on Monday. Jack was back in California. "San Francisco?" I said to Kevin. "What the hell is Jack doing in San Francisco?" It was supposed to be Westport House, airport, San Diego.

It ended up Westport House, Kevin's, airport, San Francisco? What the heck is he doing in San Francisco? Same thing, Jack convincing and manipulating.

I was grocery shopping at Stew Leonard's. It is the largest dairy store in the world, or something like that. One must push the cart in one direction, there was no going back. They have everything there, so it was a little busy to say the least. Stuffed cows walk around and talk to the kids, or a country band of milk and broccoli with fiddles and banjos sings songs about healthy food. It's noisy.

My phone rang. "Jack" appeared on the screen.

"Jack, what are you doing in San Francisco? It is Emily's birthday, you are supposed to be in San Diego."

He said he was picking up his surfboard from his friends (he had been there a couple months before), and he was staying a couple of days to surf. That was not the plan!

"How are you getting to San Diego?" He said his friend was driving him. That was not cool, I didn't trust this kid. The last time he was in San Francisco, he and this same kid drove Jack's truck out to some place to "look at the stars," and who knows what else. I received a call in the early morning. They had a major accident. His friend was driving, he said there was no drinking. Jack was a wreck. He said that was the closest he had ever come to death. Not really, he was always almost dying. His new truck was totaled, and he said another couple of inches and he would have lost his head. Ends up the kid fell asleep at the wheel; they were taking pills.

I told Jack I could barely hear him, that I was at Stew Leonard's shopping, and I would call him later. His voice sounded sketchy, "Are you back from Florida?" he asked.

"I just said I was at Stew Leonard's, so yes, I'm back."

He said, "I just wanted to talk to my mom, I'm so far away, what if I die surfing?"

"Why would you say that? Why would you die surfing, and why are you surfing anyway? Get yourself to San Diego, find a job, and get on with your life. You have been away for five weeks, you are not on vacation. Get home!"

I've learned since then that we have exit points that we plan into our incarnations. I can see them now, there were many for Jack. I don't know why he chose this one, or if it was an accident, but is anything accidental? I don't know. I don't know much, but I do know that at three years old Jack almost drowned when he fell between two boats. He had a gun held to his head, I just recently learned, while driving with a friend in South Norwalk. He overdosed and was revived by Narcan. He was nearly decapitated in a car crash. I find him with a needle on his bathroom floor, and now he might die surfing.

After Jack passed, I went to a shaman in Santa Fe, New Mexico. Visiting her was a part of the spiritual path I found myself on. I wanted to know if she could have helped Jack. I didn't understand the healing powers of a shaman. She helped me understand. She channeled her guides. It was pretty weird, as her body was taken over, and her voice changed to this deep monotone. They told me Jack knew he was going to die, he didn't know how or when, but he knew. He did know, he told me.

My childhood friend Lisa went on the trip with me to Santa Fe. We decided to go on a juice cleanse for the week. Bad idea, but funny. I had so much cleansing to do. Lisa and I go back to elementary school. There was a large gap in our communication when our kids were growing up. We lived in different places, developed new local friends. With a wonderful friend, you can always pick up at any time, and that's how it is with Lisa and me. This time we were hurled together, and to me, she was like sleeping on a lovely soft pillow. I could just lean back and she was behind me, supporting me.

I told Jack if he ever went into my wallet again, I would never speak to him. Idle threats, he did time and again. I tried to protect my wallet. Under the pillow didn't work, so sometimes I would stick it in the waist of my pajamas. Money always went missing. Even at my bank, he found my PIN. I don't know how, resourcefulness kicking in again. A few summers back my bookkeeper said there was a lot of cash withdrawn from my account. I told her I was spending getting the kids ready to go back to school. When I finally looked at it, I went cold. It wasn't me. I didn't ever even go to that bank. Oh no, please don't let it be Jack.

Kevin went to the bank to look at the photo; it was him.

Jack was finally back in San Diego, time to look for a job, celebrate Emily's birthday, all good. I went to pay some bills online. Time for American Express. Reviewing my statement, I saw a flight from San Francisco to San Diego charged to my card.

"You took my credit card again, are you fucking kidding me? After all we just went through! I am never speaking to you again!"

I said those words to him over the phone. That was the last we spoke.

I still think of him every time I go to my online banking and have to put in my PIN. I've changed it so many times, cancelled my credit cards many times. I feel he is looking over my shoulder, that he knows my new PIN.

*Jack and Emily,*
*San Diego, Fall 2014*

*November 2, 2015*

*Dear Jack,*

*I am home now, it is very very hard to be here. The light framed my door last night while I was awake at three in the morning. I always kept the door closed and never felt you were safe until that light was out. At four when the light was still on I found you. I was so afraid, if I didn't find you, you probably would have died then. You told me, "If this happens again I am going to die." You knew and you told me. I didn't do enough. You told me again when in San Francisco that you might die surfing, why were you there? Just to get pills? You missed Emily's birthday. You told me you were going to die and I didn't hear you. Everyone told you you would go to jail or die and now you're dead.*

*April 15, 2015*

*Dear Jack,*

*My hand can barely hold a pen. I can't see the page through my tears. NO NO NO Jack, Why? Why? I can't even write but I want to talk to you. All my letters just didn't matter, my love for you is crossing through time and life. I am trying to reach you so you know how much I miss you. I don't know who that was who lied to me, stole from me and frightened me, but I do know my baby, my love, my Jack. So big and strong and why? So much to offer, so much ahead of you and now you're gone. I am so sad. I look at your sweet face in photos - sweet eyes, cutest smile. I was on Team Jack. I would do anything for you. You wouldn't stop - couldn't stop. I don't know. Is it better now, better than being with us? With the ocean? With those who love you? Will we ever know? I don't see any signs where should I look?*

*We are so sad without you.*

*Come to me please, so I can hold you and tell you I'm sorry for not doing more. What could I do? What could I do? I am so sad without you. Sometimes I think I can go on and other times I can't. The drugs were like the devil. I fucking hate the devil.*

*Fuck you demons and dealers and predators that stole my son. Fuck you, fuck you! I hate you. Leave my family alone - leave my babies. They are mine to care for and I couldn't. I am sorry Jack, I am sorry Harry, I love you so much, I am sorry, I am sorry.*

*April 30, 2015*

*Dear Jack,*

*Tomorrow it will be one month, I can't get up. I am so sad. I cry over your grave, I can barely see this page through my tears. You are supposed to be here holding me up, but you are gone. I don't feel your presence and I feel like each day is getting worse and worse. I am so heart broken. I see pickles in the store and remember you said you liked them, I got them for you. Now when I see them I think of you. You always wanted lunch when you were here and there isn't any food where you are. No food for my baby, how could that be.*

*I am in such despair, my family and my friends are so good to us but it doesn't help at all. I wish I could share this grief with Dad but I am alone. Grace, Will, and Henry are much stronger than me. My heart has been broken so many times and this time it is in pieces just like Humpty Dumpty, it can't be put back together.*

*When will I see you, I miss you but at least I don't feel fear. With you, I was always afraid. When you were using you always lied to me and stole from me, but like Grace said, you were like a puppy and we would always forgive you, even when you were bad.*

*I am so sad it hurts. I hate waking up every day.*

*November 11, 2016*

*Dear Jack,*

*I am in Santa Fe with Lisa. We are trying to detox. Remove past traumas that have been trapped in the cells and organs in our body. In yoga they are called samskaras. Sounds like some scars. I have too many to count. I can't sleep. Lisa slept the entire night without even moving. Not me. When awake I feel sad and worried and afraid. All these emotions I am trying to get rid of. Nothing works. I am alone and don't know where my future lies. Hopefully this week will give me some clarity.*

*Art Journal page, No More Tears*

# MEDIUMS, INTUITIVES AND SHAMAN, OH MY!

My first visit to a medium was with Anna Raimondi in Wilton, Connecticut. My friend Suellan set up a meeting for June 22, 2015, I remember, it was a Monday.

Suellan is a long-time friend from Connecticut. She lived with her family on the next street, right on the water, Rocky Point Road. Suellan knows everything. And if she doesn't, while you are asking the question, she is simultaneously Googling it to find the answer. Will says she is like a human App on an iPhone.

My small dog was having seizures, so I took him to the vet and they put him on medication for life. Suellan said I should feed him grain free dog food. I did and he is no longer on the meds and has been seizure free for three years. When I was overwhelmed that my rusted lampshade by my bed needed to be removed, she saved the day. I thought I would have to remove the fixture from the wall, so I would need an electrician, then a painter. Too much, I never did it. While I was telling her about it, she went to my room and simply removed the shade.

There's the time I was on a spring break trip with Grace and a friend to Atlantis. I was sitting by the pool alone, phone rings, it's Jack. His high school spring break was different than Grace's. Jack and Kevin got in a fight while driving, Kevin stopped the car (this was a classic move), and Jack got out and started to walk.

"Jack, what am I supposed to do about it? I'm in the Bahamas."

I called Suellan, and she picked him up. I then called the waitress over for a rum drink.

When I arrived at the reading, Anna, the medium, said, "I don't make appointments on Mondays, how did you get this one?"

"I don't know, my friend made it for me," I said.

I didn't know what to expect. I felt somewhat prepared from watching mediums on YouTube and opening the conversation to others who knew more than I did. I was nervous, though. Would I actually communicate with Jack? What if he doesn't come through?

Anna said that during the reading she scribbles on paper. She said it was energy, a representation of it. I looked at what she drew, and it was just how my brain felt at that moment. All scrambled up, thoughts bumping into others, chaos and confusion. That was my brain illustrated.

After a few moments of drawing, she spoke again, identifying my son. She said he must have just passed because he didn't have the energy to "come through" (part of the terminology that has become my vernacular). He was only able to come through because he was with my dad. My dad? She said he was so dapper, like Fred Astaire. He would have loved that description. And yes, my dad was so dapper, won best dressed in New York City twice by the *Daily News Record*, the men's fashion newspaper. Weekends were spent in corduroys, cashmere socks and a sweater, brown suede loafers, maybe even an ascot. He sported longish hair and a gray beard. Yeah, he was dapper all right. She said, "He had a K name like Ken, Kenny." Right again. My dad is Kenny Bates, dapper, Kenny. Oh, and she loves his accent, asking, "Is he Irish or Scottish?"

"Scottish," I said, through deep breaths and endless tears. My dad was with my son.

"Who is the J name?" she asked. "Like Jake or Jack,"

"That's him," I said.

"He said, that is not his full name, he has a fuller name like, Jackson."

"Yes, his name is Jackson."

"He is on a boat, fishing. He loves boating, fishing, lacrosse, skiing, snowboarding."

"It was an accident," Anna said, "he didn't mean to die."

The entire session I stared in disbelief. I could hardly see Anna's face through my tears. Jack was here, she could see him. It was so hard to grasp. So many are skeptics, but this became the beginning of my life's work, trying to reach Jack. It started before his death, probably four years prior, when things were getting bad, when he was disconnecting from the family, from me. I would write letters, always starting the same way, "Dear Jack," just like I did when he was a baby. A desperate plea from a mother trying to reach her son. The mission never stopped, and it hasn't stopped now.

Anna went on to say, "He loves loves loves Grace, who's Grace?"

"That is his sister," I said.

She asked who Kevin was, and she talked about Will and his music and Henry at school. She told me I needed to see a doctor. I was taping the conversation on my phone and the phone rang when she was talking about Henry. The name Dr. Gordon came across my phone. My doctor was calling me? She had never done that. I answered and it was the office calling, the assistant telling me I needed to set up my annual appointment. They have never done that before. That was so weird. Anna said there are no coincidences, and especially not in her office. We continued on with the reading. She told me I needed to go to Scotland, and see the M name, which is my dad's cousin, Margaret. She said Jack and my dad would go with me. A year later, Grace and I headed to Scotland. We rode horseback through the endless herds of sheep, up the hills through the heather. We went to see Margaret. I needed a hug.

When I left Anna's office, I went straight to Dr. Gordon's office because they said they could see me that day. I was sitting on the cot waiting for Dr. Gordon.

She came in and said, "I didn't see you on the schedule,"

"I wasn't," I said. "Your office called me."

She said, "That's weird, we don't do that."

I told her the conversation with Anna. She believes in it, spirits and psychics. She said it started for her when her husband died a few years back. We chatted about the supernatural, the spirits of our loved ones, and how to reach them. Listening to my stories in her white lab coat, with her stethoscope around her neck and her reading glasses on her nose, she brought out her prescription pad and wrote down the name of a psychic. I went.

I became obsessed with books, YouTube videos, blogs, everything on life after death. I watched the TV series *Life after Death*, for example. A detective hosted this show. I am not sure why he originally started it, but he interviews psychics and the like.

I also liked "Channeling Erik." I read the blog and watched all the YouTube videos. It was the story of the son of Elisa Medhus, MD, a mother of five who lives in Texas. Her son, Erik, took his own life years back when he was in his early twenties. She wrote a book entitled *My Son and the Afterlife*. A woman named Jamie Butler from Atlanta "channels Erik." His spirit speaks through her about his afterlife experience. He describes in detail what the transition was like, the fact that time is not linear, the life review. He describes the life review as looking at a quilt—you can see the whole thing at once but it is made up of little pieces put together, scenes of your life. He says it is more about how you made other people feel, and how they felt about you. Most importantly, there is no judgement. It was and is fascinating. I continue to follow "Channeling Erik" on Facebook, along with hundreds of thousands of followers.

I watched endless videos on group and private readings with other mediums, including John Edwards, Jamie Butler, and Lisa Williams. The experience was real. Not by accident, I found myself surrounded by like-minded people. What I have learned is that what you put out there is returned to you.

Spending the summer after Jack's passing on Martha's Vineyard, holy ground, my healing place, I took refuge. I practiced yoga on my own, walked on the beach, feet in the hot sand and cooling ocean. I ate organic foods, and the local catch of the day. I felt the healing power of Martha. Friends who loved and cared about me showed up for a visit. It was a true gift to have that time to heal.

One night I was awake in my bed. My night light was to the right of me, plugged into the wall. I glanced at it, it was kind of bright. I had thought on occasion to take it out, the kids had taken out all of the others. But I didn't, I kept mine. It was bright and then it darkened and lit, darkened and lit, as though something covered it for a second, back and forth. I believe it was Jack. I knew he was still here.

I did a lot of reading over that summer, but my taste in books had changed. From *Fifty Shades of Grey*, or *The Girl with the Dragon Tattoo*, to *The Anatomy of the Sprit*, by Carolyn Myss, or *Your Soul's Plan*, by Robert Schwartz, agreements made before you were born. Yes, that's reading on a whole new level. Another favorite is *The Afterlife of Billy Fingers*, a conversation with a sister and her dead brother from heaven. It was all consuming, it was all I read and watched, it was all I talked about and listened to.

Searching the web for more information, I headed to the Lisa Williams website. I watched her recorded sessions many times and loved her approach to mediumship. She had a British accent and a big smile. She ended every session with a giant hug. I checked her availability and her next opening for a reading was September 2, Jack's birthday. I took the appointment and hoped to have the rest of the family on the call, or call in. Once again, with accuracy, we had the reading. It took place over the phone. Will and Grace sat with me and we all listened in together. Kevin called in, Henry didn't. That's ok. I know they think I'm crazy, but I don't care.

Back to real life, my home in Connecticut, a place that was haunted by grief, fear and pain. Everyone was where they were supposed to be. Will was in Nashville, music music music. Henry was in Boston at Northeastern University, studying business and finance. Grace was now a freshman at University of Denver, and Jack was in Heaven. Is that where he was supposed to be? And I was alone, in that big house. No, it didn't feel right. Off I went, back to Martha's Vineyard. I felt safe there. Get me back on that ferry!

Things quieted down on the island in September, but it could not have been more beautiful. Continuing with my yoga practice and walking on the beach, where I could even bring my dogs now that the summer season was over. Things were different on the beach in September, all the rules changed. No beach stickers, no clothes, dogs, surfers, the locals were in full swing. I had never been on the island in the fall. Kids back to school, activities, sports. Before there was no time for that, but now the kids were older and away. So many activities and opportunities for learning and creating on this magic island.

Grabbing my coffee, I would begin my day writing. "Dear Jack," my journal continued, my communication with my son never stopping. Following journaling came my readings, my book on grief and loss, my meditation book titled *Streams in the Desert*, a daily devotional. This is a left over from my recovery from Harry's death. I didn't find it helpful anymore. I watched a YouTube video, or read a blog, one like "Channeling Erik." Meditation, alone or guided, followed by a gentle yoga practice. My days had changed from getting everyone up and out of bed in the mornings, off to school, beds made, shopping, preparing dinners. It was just me and Jack now.

I have a small shed in the back of my cottage in Menemsha. It was filled with paint cans, nuts and bolts, bikes, a wagon filled with beach toys, beach chairs, boogie boards, surf boards. I wanted to empty it for a while, and then I finally did. Aparigraha, the virtue of non-hoarding. Aparigraha is a teaching in the Sutras of Patanjali, an Indian sage who wrote the Yoga Sutras, guidelines for living a purposeful life. We read through all the teachings in the yoga teacher training I assisted with Sherry. Like most things yogic, aparigraha means more than just getting rid of a collection of stuff. It is the hoarding of the energy in the room, hoarding the space or a conversation. The stuff in the shed had to go. I hired someone to take it to the dump. Painted the floor light gray, the walls white. I found a cool arched window at a wrecking shop, it had a B right in the center. Well, that must be mine then. I created my yoga studio. My sacred space.

For years, Will would sit in the tiny backyard of the cottage and play his guitar, saying, "Mom, this is the coolest spot, we need to make something back here, chairs or something." I didn't see it. Every summer he would suggest it, but I didn't see it. You see it when you see it. Two summers ago I saw it. My mind was always so filled with fog. As it started to fade, I saw it. I surprised Will by building a small patio. I had beautiful sofas built out of old barn wood, ordered cushions and a fire pit. The patio is attached to my now yoga studio. We had a sanctuary. Thank you, Will.

*My sanctuary, Menemsha, Martha's Vinyard*

*May 20, 2015*

*Dear Jack,*

   *I think you were here last night. We did it all wrong, you needed a spiritual healer. I didn't know, I would have done anything for you, anything. Why did I not know this spiritual world? Demons had you. I hate them and I am going to war with them, and I am going to find you. My love for you will transcend this life into yours.*

   *I have to correct issues with me in order to be clear to be with you. And when I die, please meet me and I won't be afraid. We were on bad terms, the drugs separated us. You were messing with the little light in my room.*

   *I know it was you.*

*Art Journal page, Perfectly Centered*

*Art Journal page, Horror*

134

# I'M NOT AFRAID OF ANYTHING

I remember when I finally identified the emotional source of stomach pain, tight chest, difficulty breathing, shaking. I thought it was anxiety, heart problems, confusion. It wasn't. It was fear. For a very long time I lived with fear. It didn't help to define it, but that is what it was.

Fear started after Harry died. Lisa my dear friend, reminded me just the other day that it started way back then, twenty four years ago. She reminded me that we visited her and her family in Orient, New York one summer. The kids were in the water, Willie and Jack and her kids. I told her I was always afraid that something would happen to my other kids. I watched, fearful, as little heads went under the water but then popped up. That was a long time ago.

When things became confusing in my marriage and things didn't add up, events didn't sit right, I would get that feeling. Stomach butterflies, shaking hands and all the other symptoms. I realized it stemmed from a sense of feeling unsafe, that my surroundings were out of control. Not listening to my intuition, it became a way of life. I was left confused and afraid. It led me to the feeling of fear, because there wasn't any trust.

Then there was Jack. He would grab money from my wallet then stare me right in the eyes and tell me it wasn't him. He lied about everything, even things that didn't matter. It became his way of life. It led me to the feeling of fear, because there wasn't any trust.

I was afraid for me and for Jack. It didn't seem to bother him though, he wasn't afraid of anything. All the trouble with the law, trouble in school, lawyers, doctors, the pending possibility of him going to jail, or dying. He never seemed afraid. I got to a point where it wasn't fear I was feeling, it was terror.

When the house phone would ring or I would get a text, or when my

*135*

cell phone rang and Jack's name came up, it triggered that fear. Often times it would start with stomach pain, then I would run to the bathroom and empty the contents of my digestive system. Fear resulted in real physical symptoms. I told my doctor my situation and she gave me Klonopin, 2.5 mg, a low dose. Just what we needed in the house. Jack found them and ate them all. He denied it.

Later, on a shaman retreat to Beverly Hills, one of our retreat leaders asked us a question. "What are we most afraid of?" Listening to everyone's answers, fear of suffering, fear of dying, fear of flying, he reaches me.

"I'm not afraid of anything."

*Art Journal page, Wear Your Freedom*

*March 20, 2016*

*Ananda Hum, I am pure joy.*

    *Well I don't feel like that. I have been treated badly and I am hurt inside no matter the time that goes by. I still feel it, it is painful to be betrayed, you don't know who to trust. Why did I go on with these total lies? It wasn't fair. I know life isn't fair, but I got it really bad. I tried to live my life respectfully, with integrity, hard work, love and caring but maybe not. I feel like I am trustworthy, but who then do I trust with my life, my heart and soul. I have been shaken to the core, my heart ripped from its place of rest. Ananda Hum, I don't think so.*

*May 8, 2016*

*It's Mother's Day. What kind of mother am I? I have tried to hold my family together and I am actually falling apart. To lose two of my children and my marriage is too much grief and sadness. All the Facebook posts on love, strength, great moms, and then there is me. Sad, broken, no strength left. I miss Jack and I want him back. I demand resolve. There is no light here. No balance to the grief. Happy Mother's Day, I don't think so. There is nothing happy about it. I am alone, on Martha's Vineyard, crying*

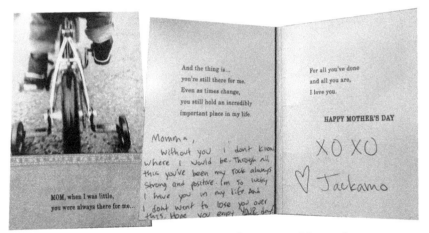

*Mother's Day card from Jack*

# SELFISH MOM

It became about my pain. How could I be so selfish? It is only now, ten months later, that I can see clearly. When I found Jack lying face down in the bathroom and lay down beside him, gasping for breath, that was about my pain. Why all the drama—my son was lying on the floor with a needle next to him, I could barely rouse him, and I started the guttural crying, the primitive roar. That was about me. Jack was the one in pain, in need. I can't even believe it, I made it about me. My suffering. What kind of mother behaves like that.

It was about my pain when Jack stole all the money from me, my pain when he stole my engagement ring. My pain and humiliation when Jack was arrested and held face down on the street in town. My pain and humiliation when the cops came to the front door to arrest him. It was my fucking pain I was worried about. My pain from the humiliation of my marital collapse, my pain from all of that hurt and embarrassment.

But Jack, he was in pain, too. That is what addiction is, a cover for pain. For Jack, it showed up as drugs, but for others it is sex, gambling, food, whatever. He was in pain. What kind of fucking mother am I who doesn't help her child who was in pain? I am forever sorry. Those extra hugs he always wanted, the tears, when he said, "Mom, I'm crying." I was so mad at him for all the trouble he caused, depleted from the cops and robbers games we played in the house everyday. I was trying to raise Grace and Henry, trying to give them a somewhat normal life, then as a single mother. Jack never followed any rules I put in place, and he would steal from me and them constantly. But it was to cover his pain, and I didn't see it. I am so sorry, I could have done more, I should have done more. Now I still have the pain, and it is deeper and longer than before. Thank God, Jack is free from his pain. I am so selfish, I am so sorry.

After writing the above entry in my manuscript, I opened my meditation book that I had been reading every morning, *Healing After Loss: Daily Meditations for Working Through Grief*, by Martha Whitemore Hickman. Judy gave it to me. She said it helped her when Andrew died.

*January 7, 2016*

*"Regret is an appalling waste of energy. You can't build on it. It is only for wallowing in."*

—Katherine Mansfield

*"Of course there are things we all regret. Things we wish we'd done differently. Even when there has been time to say all the appropriate things, images will flash in our minds that we'd give a lot to be able to change. Surely our loved one has forgiven us. Can we forgive ourselves?"*
*"I am sorry, Please know that I loved you. I know that you loved me."*

—*From Healing After Loss*, by Martha Whitemore Hickmann

All of these words of comfort I read, all the hours I spend writing, painting, practicing yoga, meditating, the support I receive from my friends and family, the mediums I speak with, the intuitives, shaman, teachers, all of it, nothing fucking works. My heart is broken in pieces. My intuitive says I am a healer. What? Me? My friend said yes, I am. I am a nurse, a yoga teacher. I studied medicinal oils and reiki, I'm a mother. Ok, I guess I am a healer. But right now, I feel it is me who needs healing. Sherry says we have to heal ourselves but it is hard, painful work. There is no way around it. It's like walking through fire. The only way out for Jack was being in a place of nothingness, nothing bothered him there, there was no pain when he was high. Just like being on a cloud, he loved it in that space, he really did, he told me. Now he is on a cloud forever, one without me.

I regret. I regret all of it.

*January 7, 2016*

*Dear Jack,*

   *I realize now how selfish I was, it became about my pain, my fucking drama and not about yours. You were in pain and I didn't see that. I only saw how you hurt me. I am a freaking selfish ass. I am just seeing this now? What is fucking wrong with me. My son is crying and in pain and I care about my fucking jewelry. Oh my God, Jack I am so sorry. I am sorry, I will be clear on that in this book I am writing, it is not about me, or Dad. It is about a little boy in pain, who was hurt. My happy bouncy little boy turned drug addict and I wasn't able to stop it. It was my fault, I'm sorry Jack. I miss you so much and will write our story for you…*

*Art Journal page, Kill Her*

*September 14, 2015*

*Dear Jack,*

*I am starting painting today. I don't know if it is going to help. Unclog blocks? My entire being is blocked despite my years of working on it. Nothing helps, but I'll try it.*

*I wish you were here with Emily and building back relationships with us. It could have happened, you needed to do the work. It has worked for others Jack. I know it was an accident, you didn't want to die, I don't think so.*

*I wish you didn't.*

*Sybil painting*

*Grace and friends art journaling and making cookies, December, 2015*

# IMAGES AND WORDS

Towards the end of the summer of 2015, I had exhausted myself, the grief, the tears, so much sadness. I felt I needed to get it out. I said to myself, I need to paint! I wanted a huge canvas to splash paint all over like blood. As these things go, I mentioned it to my friend Monique. She said her daughter just spoke with an intuitive painter here on Martha's Vineyard and gave me her business card: Melissa D'Antoni. I called right away.

She told me about an upcoming retreat here on the island in September. I told her I didn't know how to paint. No skill required.

I thought I should briefly tell Melissa my current emotional state. I told her about Jack, my grief. She said, "I know all about you, my good friend Michael James told me." Michael James, what? That is so weird. I immediately texted him. He said, "Barbara, I told you all about her at your house following Jack's service." I don't remember anything.

Our first evening we had an opening circle with all the participants, the old familiar circle. Melissa announced that she was pregnant and she hadn't told anyone, someone else had no children, I was grieving the loss of a child, then Sybil... She was sitting next to me offering tissues, then she starts crying too, saying her family was a mess, her children are challenging. She went into brief detail. When it was all over, I went up to her and said, "I feel like I need to give you a hug," and I did. She said, "Do I know you?" "I don't think so." She said it more than once. I don't remember meeting her anywhere before. She is a little southern spitfire from Savannah, Georgia. "Dude," she called me. She was colorful, funny, stylish. I did feel like I knew her. I know her now, we are tight.

The next day we were ready to paint. We were in a big open barn with a large table in the center of the room cluttered with brushes of all sizes and shapes. Paints in every color imaginable, primary, pastels, neon, glittered. Along the walls were huge papers forming stations for all of us. Melissa had a sand timer in her hand. She said she would turn it over and it would last ten minutes. We were to fill our dishes, or whatever they are called, oh, pallets, with paint and JUST PAINT. "Do not stop moving your hand until the sand timer is out," she said.

GO!

What the heck? I didn't know what to do. There were artists in the group. It was actually harder for them, used to color and composition and all of that. I just started swishing my brush around and around, splatting the paint, dabbing the paint, it didn't matter, it had to come out.

What a great retreat. It was exhausting though. It was from nine in the morning until eight at night for seven days. We painted all day. We were fed artisan meals and had great story time. The one thing I didn't like was "morning movement." Dancing around like a hippy. Not for me. I didn't feel like dancing. I didn't like morning movement, but I did it anyway, anything to facilitate my healing. Sybil always made me laugh. She had some great moves, hot momma, but she didn't like morning movement, either.

We were not allowed to finish a painting without a review. We needed to speak with Melissa about our feelings, and she would encourage us to go deeper, to investigate the shapes and colors on the paper. When we were done, we signed the painting and left it to dry.

So, I'm painting away (no talking, no music) and all these bright colors are looking happy, and annoying. I told her I wanted to start a new painting.

"No," she said. "Let's look at it. So, what is it that is bothering you?"

"I hate this painting," I said.

"Why?"

"Because it is all bright and happy and I don't feel that way."

"How do you feel?"

"I feel sad."

"What color is that?" she said.

"Gray."

"Ok, then add gray."

I really wanted to rip up the paper, but I went for the gray paint. I covered the whole thing with gray and kept going. I placed a big gray heart in the middle that was broken. I then took red paint and slashed the brush and threw paint on to the paper. I took the black paint and painted FUCK YOU across the page.

It was time for review. She said, "Is it finished?"

"Yes," I said.

"How do you feel?"

"Better."

"Sign your name."

I stumbled upon another workshop up island in Chilmark, a creative writing workshop. I passed the sign often, but never gave it a thought. Writing from the heart, with author Nancy Aronie. I signed up. I also told Sybil about it, and she signed up too. When people asked what we do, we just said, "We go to workshops." Our bond continued to thicken with the deep work we were doing. This workshop was not as intense as the painting workshop, half days during the week. Same basic instruction as PAINT. WRITE. Does anyone give instructions? Write, and don't stop moving the pen.

We were instructed to write from a prompt. I never did that before, but I never painted before, either. Like the painting workshop, where there were actually painters/artists, there were writers in the class, so descriptive, funny and tragic. Everyone has a story, life is hard.

There were twenty five in the group and we started in a circle (I was a pro at this by then), sharing a little of our background with the group. It all seems vague now. Everything from that summer is vague. There were all shapes and sizes at this workshop. Some islanders, some from afar.

Our first prompt was "Dinner at my house…" That was not tragic for me. I have the fondest memories of dinner at my house when I was growing up. I am certain they were not all butterflies and roses, but that's how I remember them. Sunday dinner: roast beef, had to be rare or my dad threw a fit, Yorkshire pudding, had to be quick because they deflate, Brussels sprouts, nobody liked them, and roasted potatoes, the neutral item on the plate.

Dinner was early afternoon, and my siblings and I were all in attendance. Not because we had to be there, we wanted to be there. My parents let us drink red wine at the table, which my friends thought was cool. The kids cleaned up. Pretty standard.

We had to read our stories out loud. Some were funny, but most terrifying. We laughed and cried and supported each other. I don't know how to write, or paint. I actually don't know much, I have come to realize. I do know how much I love my children. I do know how appreciative I am to be walking this path, this journey of seeking, reaching and longing. Once the class was over, we ate hot freshly baked bread, butter and jam. The best part!

Sybil is hilarious, I crack up at most everything she says. Oh my God, laughter. It had been so long since I laughed and laughed and laughed until I met her. She has a true gift. Over the months, we became soul sisters. The amazing thing was that in the short time since we met, her life flip-flopped. She told me her family and in-laws were all going on a Disney cruise in February. I scratched my head. This fragile, afraid, repressed young lady, who was considering a life without her family, had trouble with her father-in-law, and was at the end of her rope, was going on a Disney Cruise with them?

"What the heck Sybil, what happened?"

"It was my intuitive, Shawn."

"Give me her number!"

Tonight's writing assignment: "What I didn't tell you then…"

*October 5, 2015*

 *I didn't tell you that when faced with trauma a part of the soul detaches from the rest. The luminescent Divine being cannot withstand the impact and resides outside the body and cannot get back in. For the soul to be reunited, to be whole again, an ancient tradition of healing is warranted. I didn't tell you shaman are healers. They have access to and influence in the spirit world. Their Divine powers can retrieve the defected soul pieces to complete you.*

 *I didn't tell you because I didn't know.*

 *I didn't tell you that in Brazil shaman provide ceremony, ancient culture, and catharsis for the soul with a hallucinogenic, heave producing, high ball that cleanses the soul while you trip your fucking brains out. I didn't tell you because I didn't know, I wonder if you did.*

 *I didn't tell you that there is something called past life regression. That the many lives we have lived leave karmic patterns that can be cleansed, one can stop patterns from continuing. Wisdom traditions use techniques including hypnosis to recover past memories and unresolved issues, and bring them to a present state of awareness and consciousness.*

 *I didn't tell you because I didn't know.*

 *I didn't tell you that the chemical make up of the brain changes with drug use. That no matter how many meetings, how many sponsors, how many rehabs, it was not going to work. It is not that you wouldn't stop. You couldn't stop.*

 *I didn't tell you because I didn't know and now it's too late and I am sorry.*

Interesting how this path leads. We cannot see what lies ahead as much as we can see where we came from. I found out about the Chilmark writers workshop from a friend I bumped into on Martha's Vineyard. She took the class and said it was wonderful and filled me in on a few details. I wasn't sure I was ready, sounded like it would be very emotional for me. I did it and it was emotional. When I completed the course, I emailed her to tell her how much I enjoyed it. I didn't hear back for a while but when I did, she said she was sorry she didn't get back to me right away, that she was teaching at an art journaling weekend and was so busy. Art journaling? What's that? She sent me to a web site dirtyfootprint-studios.com. This page contained instructions from twenty-one artists detailing different techniques for art journaling.

This was perfect! I can't paint or write, but I can cut and paste. I ordered my journal, all the paints, tempera and water color, big sheets of paper, too. Glue, scissors, markers were delivered and I converted half of my yoga shed into an artist studio. Brushes in cute jars, pallets, all of it. I got right to work.

I would sit for hours. Painting, cutting out bits of magazines expressing my feelings or thoughts, pasting them in my art journaling book. When the season on Martha's Vineyard ended, I brought it all home. I covered my dining room table with plastic, set up my paints and brushes and continued the craft. I invited my yogi girls over one day. We made pizzas, and afterwards I laid out big sheets of paper and magazines and they did amazing work. That made me happy. And for Christmas, Grace and all her girl friends baked cookies and then hit the dining room for the same creative process. Amazing creativity and expression of thoughts and feelings. (Especially after a case of champagne.) I don't remember having this kind of outlet as a teenager. I don't think I even needed it.

*October 21, 2016*

*Dear Jack,*

*It is a beautiful day on Martha's Vineyard. Warm, trees are turning colors. I've never been here this time of year. Are you with me? I need to speak to a medium again so I can talk with you? Why can't you talk to me? Why do I need someone else? You know you are in my head and heart constantly.*

*I hear nothing back. No whispers or wiping my tears away. Me alone crying, writing, reading, journaling, painting, and walking, trying to stay alive for Will, Henry and Grace. Sometimes I don't want to. It is way too tough, too sad.*

*My intuitive painting*

*Art Journal page, Healing*

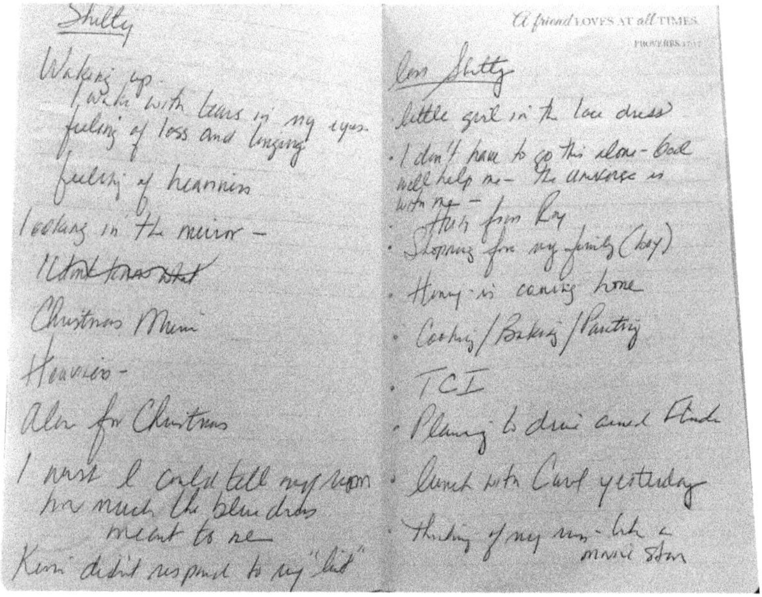


Shitty and less shitty, prescribed by Shawn Phelps

# INTUITION

Shawn Phelps is an intuitive from Ontario, Canada. Sybil gave me her number. Intuitives have a knowing... They have insight into areas of a person's life the person can't see for themselves. She offered a fifteen-minute free Skype or phone consultation to see if there was a fit between her and her client. I signed up. Our first session lasted one and a half hours, not fifteen minutes. She said that we are in this life to experience JOY. What the heck is that? Joy? I don't know what that looks like. Well, actually I do, I saw it in Sybil. Ok, I want some of that, tell me what to do.

During the brief amount of time that I spent working with Shawn, my life dramatically changed. She read my spirit and received messages from my true self, versus some of the other psychics and intuitives I've spoken with, who receive messages from spirit or spirit guides. She told me my lesson to learn in this lifetime was self-minimalization. You mean like being a doormat? She told me my life's purpose was to be a healer. That didn't resonate with me. I didn't feel like a healer, I still felt like I needed to be healed.

I do everything Shawn tells me to do. It is homework, work. It is not a day at the spa. That's what it means to take care of yourself. This is painful work and I do it every day. With my hand on my heart, I talk to my little girl self, my true essence, out loud. Shawn called this the wise parent exercise, telling my child self that she is safe and that we will step into this day holding hands and skipping. Entering the day with ease and joy.

Then there was the celebration log, where I celebrate something, any-thing, like when I put on lipstick. Then I write the negative comment, which could be, "You still look bad," and rephrase it to something positive, "I am trying to bring color to my face."

Then there was the evidence log. Here I wrote what seemed weird, or unusual, or a coincidence. Whenever I said, "That's weird," I wrote it down.

My morning routine these days takes about four hours. That's work.

The first session I had with Shawn, she had me write two lists. One was titled "shitty," the other was "less shitty." We were starting at the bottom. I would list things that happened throughout my day that made me feel shitty. That was easy, everything made me feel that way. Less shitty challenged me to find something, anything, that made me feel less shitty. This was a shorter list. For instance, "It felt less shitty to have a warm cup of tea."

She also had me choose my Dream Team, the people in my life, other than my family, that were my go-to dependable people. It was easy to do.

Lisa, my childhood friend reentered my life in the most profound way, never leaving my side, either by a visit or a call. Suellan was there at every turn for me, whether it was listening, understanding, or the busy work of whatever needed to get done. Jen helped me to understand addiction and the role of God in our lives. Meghan, solid to the core, dependable, understanding, and funny. Sybil…what would I have done without Sybil, the laughter, the workshops. My dream girls, thank you, thank you, thank you.

It took me hours to even get out of bed doing all this work. A day never began without tears, without the longing, but I kept doing it. I didn't feel like I was getting better, but where would I be without this ritual.

With Shawn's help, I rediscovered intention. Putting your intention, or prayer, out into the universe. Our guides and spiritual friends don't know which way our free will is taking us. When we say it clearly, write it down, visualize it, it is out there and we have the support of the universe, the wind at our back.

Still on Martha's Vineyard chatting with my neighbor, Jill, she told me about two visitors coming to the island. They were shaman. I still didn't know exactly what that meant, not really, even though I visited one in Santa Fe. I was thinking indigenous tribe in Brazil or Peru, drums, nose rings, feathers. What did I know, but I was damned to find out. The shaman were coming to the island, but I wasn't able to go. Sybil and I were in the painting retreat at the same time.

Jill, I come to find out, is a healer in her own right. She feels energy. We had long talks about energy, the afterlife, astrology, and Akashic records.

What the heck is that? Our past and future lives.

A flash back to yoga class with Sherry. In downward dog, "This life, our past lives and future lives." Breathe in and breathe out. I heard her say it, "You hear it when you hear it."

I'm still working on that concept, it is freak'n out there and I need more mental capacity to wrap my head around it. What I find amazing is that this entire network of people, healers, teachers, shaman, gurus, are in our world practicing a spiritual life alongside us. I am a complete novice, or newbie, as Jack would say. I thought I was an advanced practitioner, too. Practicing yoga for fifteen years, becoming a yoga teacher. Now, I have been truly launched onto the path. There is no turning back, I will never see life the same.

Then came my session with Jamie Butler from "Channeling Erik." I had been waiting for eight months for this appointment.

Our session was to take place over the phone. I prepared my questions, had my recorder ready to tape our conversation. Then I prayed that Jack would show up. I had questions. I usually sat limp, in a puddle of tears, and listened to whatever validation came through. Not this time, I was going to be prepared and ask Jack where he was. Did he long for me like I longed for him? Did he even miss us or were all his needs met? Did he have friends there? Did he feel the love that is all that is, LOVE? I hope so—that is all there is, you know.

I was very nervous for this reading. I waited with my phone by my side, ready to tape and call in at the precise moment. I told her I was nervous. She said she was so excited to speak with me. That nine spirits showed up to communicate with me. That they said I was a wonderful person, and they said many nice things about me. I'll put that on my "less shitty" list. Jack showed up, but he was not as vocal as my Auntie Kathleen, my mother's sister. She was very concerned I was open to more manipulation and lies, and that I needed to be aware. I'm aware alright. When I see crazy coming, I cross the street.

She asked the spirits in her presence where was the baby, Harry. He wasn't there. They said his spirit returned to the earth plane as Jack.

Jack and Harry were one.

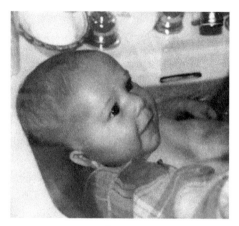

*Baby Harry*

*Art Journaling page, Heart and Light*

*Jack's shape at the end of my bed*

# DREAMS AND VISIONS

I thought I was dreaming. Was I? It happened so quickly. It must have been the early morning, but still dark. I don't know that for sure, either. It was just days since the worst fucking day in my existence. I lifted my head, and at the end of the bed was Jack. It was clear to me, it happened so fast. I opened my eyes and his shape was sitting on the end of my bed, his head in his hands. I couldn't see through him, it was his shape, I don't know how else to describe it. Then he was gone. I laid my head back down and decided it was a dream. It was days later when Grace said to me "Mom, Jack came to my room. He was standing in the doorway, I ran up to him and jumped into his arms and he buried his head in my neck. He said I am sorry, I am sorry, then he was gone. I know it wasn't a dream."

Suellan had set up the original appointment with Anna Raimondi, a psychic medium and grief counselor, without my knowledge. I wasn't even sure exactly what that was at the time. I had to wait weeks for my appointment. In the meantime, I was searching for her information/website on line. "Medium in Wilton Connecticut," I typed in. I didn't find it, but stumbled on a site for Lisa Williams, the British medium who did group readings as well as private ones. I watched the readings, I had never heard of this before. How did I not know about this world of alternative healing, of intuitives, psychics and mediums. I always had thought a psychic was more like a gypsy with a crystal ball.

There is a world of like-minded people, who practice this kind of work all over the world. It was not like one person was leading this particular technique or movement. These are ordinary men and women who read energy and can connect with the spirit world. A vernacular I was unfamiliar with, well not really, my teacher, Sherry, always would thank our guides, our swimming friends, our flying friends. Spirits in this life and past lives. I am listening, sitting cross legged, hands to heart in prayer position. Namaste.

While on a beautiful walk along Lucy Vincent Beach, barefoot along the water's edge, I walked with my teacher. She reminded me, "We hear it when we hear it," like when we are ready. I guess I'm ready.

I remembered back when I was waiting for my first appointment with Anna Raimondi, I came across a YouTube group reading with Lisa Williams and was taken aback by the accuracy of the information. The reading ended with a question and answer period. Guests could line up and ask the medium their questions. One lady walked up and described her loved one sitting at the end of her bed days after his passing. She described exactly what I saw. The medium said to her matter-of-factly, "That was him." They come to their loved ones as they have not transitioned and are still attached to this material life. That was it, and one day at a time, one book, one YouTube video, one thing then another, I was learning.

As our walk through the frothy wake of the ocean continued, Sherry said to me, "It's as though you are on a treasure hunt," and I am. I am on a hunt to reach my son.

I signed up for a shaman retreat in California with the two men Jill told me about who came to Martha's Vineyard. It was a shaman apprenticeship retreat. This was where my hunt led me. Sybil looked them up and found this retreat/workshop in Los Angeles.

It was more intense than I expected going there. I didn't anticipate that touching down at Burbank Airport would well up in me a grief so overwhelming, it left me gasping for breath. Jack loved "Cali," it was where he died. Although it was in San Diego, there was something about the air and the palm trees, it was all the same. The names like Sepulveda, Ventura, the 101, were stifling. I arrived two days before the retreat was to begin. I stayed with my friend, now dream girl, Lisa, and prepared for the coming days. I didn't know what was going to happen there.

This happened the first night at Lisa's house. It was one of those sleeps, deep and clear. Jack was there, but he was about five. He said for me to think of him at that age, happy mischievous, cheeky, not like how he ended up. He said that dark part of him died with him. In the dream, he was so clear, looking me straight in the eyes. Through sobbing tears, I said, "I miss you so much Jack." He said, "When you threw the tissue, that was me, and when you held Minnie Mouse that was me." I didn't know what that meant. Sometimes communication is unclear because it hasn't happened yet or maybe it was long ago. For spirit, time is not linear, it is simultaneous, parallel.

I reached for him, and I said, "I want to hold you," and he said, "You can't hold on to me." He said, "I need to go." Simultaneously I said, "Please don't say that," sobbing and reaching. I jumped up from bed, shouting, "Jack!"

Later that night, I fell back to sleep after what seemed like hours. Jack was back, this time older, and he was in the hospital. He was crying, and I was by his side. He was on the gurney, and I was next to him just like many years before with the wrist accident. There were tubes and blood. The doctor was crying too, lying over him. He told Jack he would be fine, that "the pendulum had stopped and he was going to go home." I woke up in a sweat, and didn't go back to sleep.

In the morning, I wrote down the above entry in my journal. It was so real. I took out my evidence log and wrote the dream in it as well, it was evidence.

The shaman retreat was the mother of all retreats. It was a trip. Well, it was not just shaman, it was Wicca, Hermetics and witchcraft. How the hell I got there was just moving myself forward. The host of the week-long retreat in Cali emailed me a few weeks before. He asked if I was still coming because I hadn't sent back my registration form. I told him that when I read in more depth the details of the retreat I felt uncomfortable. I was curious about the shaman, but other aspects of the retreat had me bumping up against my comfort zone. I wanted to make this trip to ask the shaman if he could have helped Jack. He sent me back a page of information and descriptions and told me when you bump up against your comfort zone, it is the time to break through. I sent in my form.

Shaman are people who have access to the world of good and evil spirits. From a trance-like state, they perform healing and other rituals. I experienced it firsthand. Wicca is described as a modern religion based on ancient witchcraft traditions. Hermetics is an ancient spiritual tradition that is also philosophical and magical. It is a path to spiritual growth. Lastly, witchcraft is the belief in and practice of magic by individuals. Using spells (intentions) and potions (herbs and oils) for healing and transformation. I think they should change the name from witches to healers. Just a thought.

Somewhere in between feeding the rose plants with my blood and water, the moon ceremony, and the shamanic spirit journeys, there were the healings. Dream girl Sybil, my soulmate, was the first chosen for this, um, ritual. Sybil took off her shoes and laid on the foam pad and blankets that were placed in front of our teacher. He discussed the technique and how he would heal her. He asked Sybil to choose someone from the group to participate with her in the healing, someone she trusted. That was me. He reached for a pendulum.

Wait, what? A pendulum, that was in my dream with Jack.

He held the pendulum, a silver weight suspended on a chain—when I had the dream, I was thinking a pendulum was a metronome like the one that sat on my Auntie Ella's piano clicking back and forth rhythmically—in his right hand and asked yes or no questions. The pendulum circled clockwise for yes and counterclockwise for no. For neutral it stopped completely. With the pendulum in hand he traced Sybil's body from the feet, up the legs, then he said, "The pendulum has stopped." That is exactly what the doctor said in my dream with Jack. I had no idea what it meant. I told our shaman host after the ceremony about my dream. I told him what the doctor said, that the pendulum had stopped. He said, "That means the cords are cut." The healing ceremony/exorcism was to cut the cords from those who steal our energy and keep us bound. I don't want my cord cut from Jack. I'm his mom and he can take my energy. I miss him so much.

The shaman laid his hands on Sybil and started this, I can't describe it, sound in the back of his throat. He grabbed on to her shirt and pulled the cords from her body, nearly snapping her neck, grabbing her neck scarf at the same time. He performed this technique several times. I placed my hands on her pelvis and pulled the energy down her legs and out through the bottoms of her feet, removing negative energy and cleansing her body. It was hard work. It was more fun watching the Argentinian girls go through this process. The girls had a different rhythm, adding a sexy, sassy snap with attitude after each release.

After it was over, I laid next to Sybil as she wept. As we both wept. He said by healing herself she would also heal her seven-year-old son. By holding her like a mom holds her child, I healed myself and I healed Jack.

The rest of the retreat weekend introduced us to more interesting rituals. We were introduced to our personal magnetic rocks, mine was named Leo! He had to be anointed with oil and dusted with metallic dust. And, by the way, I had to dust him and talk to him once a week.

Then came the money bag dressed in red silk…I forget what I'm supposed to do with that, I think droplets of whiskey.

The purpose jar I had to leave behind. It was a baby food jar, in it a snip of my hair (which when cut, disrupted my new high-low hairstyle), a fingernail clipping, my intention of JOY written on paper, silver sparkles that act like mirrors, lots of herbs and filled with honey. That jar is to be shaken once a week to the east and then a candle is supposed to be burned on top. I didn't want to check my bag on the flight home, and I couldn't really explain to the security guard at the airport check-in what the magical jar was. I decided to leave it in Lisa's bedroom that I shared with her daughter.

In the days ahead, Lisa's daughter's life changed dramatically. She moved from Los Angeles to San Francisco, accepting an amazing job that had hundreds of applicants. I guess they can keep the jar. I'll have to tell Lisa you can't throw it out, you have to bury it. I don't know if it is to the east or west.

There was also the magic bag filled with all the ceremonial materials we used throughout the week. It was supposed to go under our pillow at night, but I was too scared to try it.

I met my power animal on the shamanic journey. We all laid down while our shaman drummed and imagined ourselves walking down steps under a tree. The first animal we met would be our power animal and companion on the rest of the journey. A fox showed up for me. He could talk, something like the beavers in Narnia. When I told Sybil, she asked, "Was he wearing a red vest?"

Without levity, I never would have made it. Rituals, spells, exorcism like healings, repeated mantras and chants, lighting candles and staring at the moon. Thank God for Sybil, she is the funniest person I know. We sat side by side during our twelve-hour days, and I never stopped giggling.

Our shaman said he does work with addicts. They do crazy exercises like hanging them off rock ledges and burying them alive so they stare death in the face. He said that then there is free will. His answer to my deepest question, "Could you have helped Jack?" was "I don't know."

The week concluded, and we graduated from shaman apprenticeship school. I wouldn't have missed it for the world. Not leaving any stone unturned, my treasure hunt. Dinner with Lisa and Sybil at the end of the week was a highlight. What are the chances, two of my major dream girls in Los Angeles at dinner together? This was not by chance. "I am going to jot this down in my evidence log."

I wanted to talk to Jack on my own; I needed to talk to Jack on my own. They say that anyone can do it, clearing the mind, being still, looking for signs. If there is a way for a non-clairvoyant, non-clairsentient, non-clairaudiente, non-intuitive to talk to spirit, then I am going to do it. I am going to find a way.

I have followed Swedenborg's readings. He was a Swedish scientist, theologian, philosopher, mystic and author. At the age of fifty three he entered a spiritual phase, his "spiritual eyes" opened, and he could freely visit with heaven and speak with angels and spirits. He says there is a divine design. There are rules to this world like gravity for instance, and rules for the spirit world too. There is a divine order. The "veil" that is often referred to as the separation of the two realms is not something physical, but of thought. Contact is made when the mind is clear, often in dreams or even driving, a somewhat meditative state. There is a language barrier however, our human minds are so limited. It is like trying to talk to a toddler about electricity or the internet. I'm an adult and I don't even know how any of that works. Spirit can not communicate information other than what we can understand. People have pierced the veil, I have seen it first hand. I am going to keep trying.

*Art Journaling page, Love and Dreams*

*My cardinal, Jackamo*

# SIGNS, SIGNS, EVERYWHERE ARE SIGNS

Do we conjure up signs as proof that our loved ones are around us? I'm not sure. I have been told there will be many signs. Pennies from heaven? I have found pennies around, but weren't they around before? I don't know, never paid attention. Now a penny is a sign that Jack is around? I don't buy it.

Or the signs that come through electronics. Since spirit is energy, I have read that they can mess with computers, telephones, dimming of lights (that did happen!). Signs that come through the radio, hearing a meaningful message in a song, or a favorite song that we shared comes on. I want it to be true.

When spirit has enough energy, they have the ability to move objects. (Like in the movie *Ghost*, with Demi Moore and Patrick Swayze.) The pencil that wasn't there a minute ago, or keys you swear you left on the counter are on the ledge instead. That happens all the time, but I believe it has to do with my forgetfulness.

There is one thing, though, I hold it so close to my heart as a sign from Jack. Very soon after April 1, the date of Jack's passing, I was circling my kitchen counter as usual. Outside on my porch railing was a bright red cardinal. The bird was in stark contrast to the white railing and gray background of early spring. I noticed it. Then I was in my bathroom upstairs and the cardinal, I guess the same one, flew back and forth past the windows. I noticed it. I said to Suellan, "It's really weird, I have to write it down, every time I look out my window there is a bright red cardinal."

"You know what that means right?"

"No," I said.

"It is a sign that spirit is near." I looked it up.

The crimson color of the male cardinal gets our attention when nothing else can, especially in times of grief and depression. I read that cardinals appear when angels are near. So, maybe it is true. It is my sign. From that point on, I would seek my little red bird, and sure enough it appeared. Right in front of me on Martha's Vineyard. The bright red bird whose song sounds like he is saying, "cheers, cheers," is always near. When I am on a morning walk, the bird swoops down in front of me and then away into the trees. I never take my eyes off it. I stop and wait until he is out of sight, not wanting to miss a second of my time with him. Or walking up my driveway Chowder Kettle Lane, swoop, there he is. I was sitting out back in my sanctuary, looking up at an enormous tree covered in ancient vines. The top branches are bare, the vines stop short of the very top. There are no leaves on the branch either. Must be a lovely view, as that was where my cardinal was perched, observing his surroundings.

While Emily was visiting, I told her about the cardinal in my life. We were walking up the main street in Edgartown, following a rosè lunch. A bird flew in front of us, and she said, "Is that a cardinal?" (She's from California, I guess they don't have them there.) "No, that is a robin red breast," I said. Then swoop, right in front of us. We both turned to each other with mouths wide open. "That's a cardinal!"

When we arrived home, the cutest thing was happening outside my house. The cardinal was in the tree, and out flew two baby cardinals. They were playing together, flying straight up and down, flipping all over. Emily taped it.

Will took a photo of a nest he had in his back yard in Nashville. Three or four little eggs nestled in a tree. He said he saw the parents, they are cardinals. Cardinals by the way are good parents, they have equal responsibility for their young. And while most birds sing alone, the cardinal parents sing together.

I used to hate birds. My sister had a little parakeet when we lived together years ago. I told her if she let it out of the cage, I would swat at it, which would probably be the end to her little fluffy friend. But now I am in awe of birds. Not to the point that I have binoculars, but I'm on track to get the hat. I notice everything. I think that is because I finally am learning to be present, I'm awake. I watch for my cardinal every day.

When in a second psychic reading with Anna Raimondi, around Christmas

2015, she asked me what was with the blue jays. I said I did see a blue jay on my walk. She said, "Blue jays fly alone, but you will see two together." I kept my eyes peeled on my walks, but didn't see them. While sitting in my living room, which is upstairs in my Martha's Vineyard house—it's like living in a tree house up there—I was talking with Kevin. We were getting on much better now. After Jack, nothing else mattered, it all seemed so petty. It was April 1, my healing day, the one year anniversary of Jack's passing. I said, "Look there is a blue jay, right behind you." He didn't know the significance until later. The blue bird was perched right outside my window, then another one flew right next to it, and they sat together. Anna was right, I played the tape for Kevin to validate the significance of the two blue birds. Another sign?

They are a sign for my family and me. I was on the phone with Grace. She and Will were staying at Kevin's apartment right on the river. The only birds there are seagulls. While still on the line, I hear Grace say to Will, "What kind of bird is that?" he replied, "A cardinal."

I think I am going to call my little red bird Jackamo.

*July 4, 2016*

*Jack,*

*A day of celebration. I think not! A day of solemnness. A day of sorry, but maybe a day of independence for you. Was it that bad, our life together, that death was better? How can that be? I will place your ashes where we went fishing, because it was just you and me.*

*I love you Jackamo and will carry you wherever I go.*

*I saw two baby cardinals this morning, they say it's a sign. I don't know though. Are you with Papa and Harry, my baby? I wish you were here and sober with Emily and enjoying Martha's Vineyard like we used to before all of this craziness happened.*

*We are all broken apart and trying to just get through each day. Emily is coming, I got a necklace for her. I hope you like mine, it's just what you told me to wear.*

*I think I'm going to keep the ashes right over my head. I'm not sure. You'll let me know. I love you Jack. I wish I lingered in your hugs in the kitchen, but I was always mad at you for stealing, using, and lying. I wish you were my little sweet boy, I miss you Jacka.*

*My life is getting too busy. I just want to stay in bed and read and write and cry. I don't want to entertain. I still can't believe it, it can't be true.*

*First place "Rock and Roll" float*

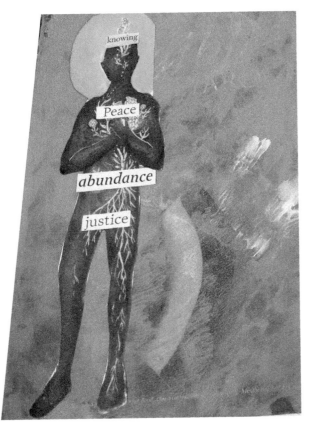

*Art Journal page, Knowing*

# INTENTION

An aim or a plan. That is intention. Seems simple.

I have sat cross-legged on my yoga mat for years. The practice begins with a grounding exercise, usually closing your eyes and focusing on your breath as the teacher speaks of a centering thought, and offers the students the space to create an intention for their practice. I never did it. I started yoga for exercise, but then found interest in the stories of all the Gods and Goddesses. I would rather grab a bolster and blanket and listen to all the versions of my self that are in the many, many deities. Story time.

Intention. This word keeps coming up. Intention seemed to me like a to-do list, and I did not need anymore to do. Then I heard it differently. (You hear it when you hear it.) Intention is the practice of removing what is standing in the way from you becoming your true self. "Remove the interference," Sherry would say. I liked that better. No more to do, just remove what is clouding your mind and body, whatever is keeping you from going into spirit and true self. Remove it.

Removing as an intention became how I taught my yoga students when I began my own teaching practice. Place your hands before your heart, close your eyes, focus on your breath. Maybe set an intention for your practice and your day. What can you remove that is preventing you from being your true self? A thought, a conversation, a worry, a relationship? Whatever it is, remove the interference.

When Sybil and I went to see the shamans of Beverly Hills, it was all about intention. So many rituals. It was complicated. Candles, a different color for every day sitting on top of our written intentions. Purpose jars that contained our intentions inside along with herbs, spit and pieces of hair and fingernail. We had to write our intentions with a nail on a tapered candle facing away from us and then our names or the name of the person who the intention was for around in a circle. Even on day seven, Sybil and I were doing it backwards. They said it didn't matter, it was our intention that mattered. It didn't matter? As long as we had the right intention? Incidents like that came up over and over again. Mistakes we were making facing east vs. west, up instead of down, the wrong herb or oil to dress our candles. It didn't matter, as long as we had the right intention. Intention can cover up a lot of mistakes.

Shawn gave me a little book called *Life's Compass* for 2016. It was a print out with questions that help guide the reader to review the previous year and put in place a plan for the next one. It included goal setting, important and meaningful thoughts. It was very helpful to me. Without forcing, it helped set up an aim or a plan for the year ahead. An intention. The last question was to write a big idea, some out of the box thing that you have considered. Write it down, go ahead! I did it, it read like this:

DARE TO DREAM BIG

What does the year ahead of you look like? What will happen in an ideal case? Why will it be great? Write, draw, let go of your expectations and dare to dream.

*Ok, I dream I could write a book-there I said it! (It was an a-ha moment.) I have a story to tell, it's mine, yes, but there are layers and layers of love and loss. Big personalities and healing in a way most of us are unaware. Deep spiritual meaning, a path that may serve others. I want to help!*

Well now we know how intention works. You write it down, you say it, and the universe is at your back. Then all we have to do is step into the flow.

*Art Journal page, Contemplation*

# APRIL 1

I miss you Jack. The morning of April 1, 2016. April Fool's Day, some fucking joke. The one year anniversary had arrived. I had written daily in my journal for a year. Two journals actually. Well four, if you count my celebration journal and evidence log. I sat in my bed on Chowder Kettle Lane surrounded by my books and journals drinking coffee. The scene was probably not much different from last April 1, a day like any other. Sipping coffee waiting to hear Grace get into the shower. She always asks for five more minutes. I went down to make breakfast. A day like any other.

The phone rang. Kevin told me. My world imploded.

It went from normal to incomprehensible so quickly. I didn't know what was going on, in shock, out of my mind. That morning my family came, I don't know who called them. Kevin came. Grace's friends came. The house was full. Oh my God.

Grace called Will and Henry. I don't know how they made it home, but they got there fast. Will flew in from Nashville, and Henry was driven home from Boston. It was catastrophic, it did not fit in my brain. I remember I kept thinking he will figure it out, he always did. He will get out of this mess and come home. You could never put Jack in a box. He was too big in size, personality, everything about him.

This devastating event did not fit in my consciousness or in my belief system. I had no choice but to expand. I needed to reach Jack. My last words to him were "I am never going to speak to you again." I told him that's what would happen if he ever took money from me again. He did, he took my credit card when he went back to California. I needed to reach him and tell him I was sorry. I didn't care about fucking money, he needed to come home.

I spent the year doing nothing but walking around in circles and going to workshops, painting, writing, shaman, mediumship, yoga. One of the greatest changes happened during my Skype sessions with my intuitive Shawn. She is an empath as well as an intuitive an author.

During the Skype session in early spring, she said she felt my heaviness so much she had trouble breathing. I was anticipating April 1, the one-year anniversary. Shawn said I needed to have a commemorative event for Jack. I was to send a Save The Date to my family, prepare invitations, make it like I was planning Grace's wedding. I was to write down my intention, which was to plan a commemorative healing event for my family and then do a visualization of what the day would be like. I hung up with her and thought to myself, there is no way I'm doing that. It's too much, I can't.

Well, since Shawn gave me the assignment of intention and visualization for Jack's anniversary, I did it. I sat in bed and wrote down my intention.

I am planning a commemorative healing event for Jack with the intention of healing myself, Will, Henry, Grace, Kevin and Emily.

There, I did it. I went to take a shower. Sitting down under the steamy water had become custom. I could be alone there and cry for as long as I wanted.

Sitting in the shower it all came to me. Flooding into my mind were the ideas for the day. And so it began. The planning. I sent the Save The Date and started invitation design.

It would be on Martha's Vineyard, the healing mecca. I'd been there the better half of that year, and the island continues to be my love. My cute, cozy house, my friends, the sand and ocean, the fresh food, even the radio station. I love MVY radio. My speakers are throughout my house, in my garden and studio. I can walk seamlessly between rooms and listen to my favorites, Neil Young, Bruce, James and Ben Taylor, Norah Jones, Jack Johnson, then jump in my car still surrounded by the same tunes. Sunday morning driving to Yoga MVY has a themed hour, "All that jazz." I love it all. It is a healing island. It is Happy Vineyard, and the perfect place for my day of healing. There are so many healers here too. I called on them and like magic the event came together. I called for reflexology, craniosacral massage, Jin Shin Jyutsu, all healing practices with the intention of healing my family.

I started getting nervous as the date grew closer. I put so much effort into making this event happen. Grace had to fly in from Denver, Will from Nashville, Henry and Emily were close in Boston. Kevin would be coming. It didn't matter, we all needed healing. Will didn't want to participate, he felt he needed to be alone, but I am glad he decided to come. I wanted to let everyone do whatever they thought was best for them, come or not come, but Shawn said no, I needed to create space for them, then they could do whatever they wanted within the space. Will ended up participating the entire day.

Flights, ferries, opening the house early, plumbers, electricians, painting, that was all under way leading up to the date. Still nervous, but I would just breathe into it and it would go away. I called dream girl Meghan. I asked if she would help facilitate the event so I could participate as well. "Of course, I would love to." I knew it.

Invitations are in the mail:

A COMMEMORATIVE DAY *of* HEALING

APRIL 1

CHOWDER KETTLE LANE

Everyone arrived the evening before. We had dinner together at the table. I gave a brief description of how the day was planned, and what my intention was.

And then it was here, April 1. I had some excited anticipation for the day ahead, like birthday mornings or Christmas mornings. I would always be up ahead of everyone, either blowing up balloons or wrapping gifts. This day began with me and my coffee, contemplating what was to come with excitement. I don't know why, but I picked up my journal and wrote big and bold,

April 1, **HAPPY BIRTHDAY JACK!!**

It was a new kind of birthday, a rebirth day.

*179*

# DAY OF HEALING

Breakfast options included acai smoothies, fresh local eggs, fresh baked vineyard bread, and Gray Barn organic farm fresh cheese.

Shamanic Stone Ceremony–Squibnocket Beach. We went to the ocean, despite the pouring rain. Privately everyone picked up a good size stone, and was instructed to talk to it and release feelings of regret, guilt, anger, whatever those feelings are that don't serve us. We then threw the stones into the water, thanking the stone and water for facilitating our healing. (Kevin and Emily dove into the frigid water with their stones.)

Restorative Yoga. Jeannie set up my shed in the back with blankets, blocks, and bolsters for restorative yoga. We did three poses in an hour and a half. She spoke gently about the healing the practice offered and introduced healing crystals into the practice as well. Restorative yoga soothes the nervous system, encourages mindfulness, deepens awareness and introspection. The practice helps one to feel safe and nurtured. We finished by holding hands with a rose quartz in the palms of our hands. Beautiful.

For lunch we went vegan, had the meal dropped off so I could participate in the healing. Kombucha to drink with teas and lemon water.

The afternoon consisted of healings set up in the bedrooms of my tiny house. There was a practitioner in every room. Each family member had a schedule to follow to participate, if they chose, in the healings.

Reflexology was offered. An alternative medicine using pressure on hands and feet to hasten healing, improve circulation, promote relaxation and toxin removal. It also stimulates the nervous system.

Craniosacral massage, a sensitive and deeply healing modality. With a gentle touch the therapist monitors the rhythm of the cerebrospinal fluid throughout the body. Sources of stress are released to help facilitate the body's amazing ability to self heal.

Jin Shin Jyutsu is the art of harmonizing the life energy. An ancient disarming form of acupressure, working with twenty-six points along energy pathways. When the pathways become blocked, energy stagnates.

Reiki is a practice of energy transfer from the practitioner to the client to improve life force energy, acting as a conduit to remove negative energies for healing.

There was a scheduled free choice time, which included painting or yoga in the shed. There was also time for a guided meditation (I used Oprah and Deepak) in Grace's tiny bedroom, where I made an altar with photos and special symbols of Jack. We put our crystals there, too. The meditation time doubled as a time for the kids to smoke weed, I think.

I left a journal in the room and called it, Writing From The Heart, if anyone wanted to express themselves that way. We would later burn the pages, the smoke our prayer.

I ordered white terry robes embroidered with a navy blue tuna fish on the left chest, which is now "Jack's fish." It was his tattoo. Now my family, cousins, and friends have them. I have it, too. On the arm, down the leg and across the chest, we are on Team Jack. Lanyards from Shatterproof, the organization we support, a force of nature helping those suffering from addiction, held the laminated schedules. Little white slippers, fire on, healthy snacks and tea. Water and candles in all the rooms.

It was awesome.

Things to note if planning such an event:

Someone needs to facilitate. I had dream girl Meghan on my team. She helped practitioners in, cleaned up, facilitated the day anyway she could. It was a tremendous help.

I encouraged everyone to drink lots of water to flush the system throughout the day. I didn't listen to my advice and drank Rosé instead.

Just provide space, no expectations. When the day was over, we stayed in our robes and slippers. Dinner was dropped off again and we added some local fish on the grill.

Will bought Macallan scotch. He poured each of us a shot.

To Jack!

I am not sure the result of the healing. For me, I stayed on Martha's Vineyard for a couple of weeks, crying for days. I supposed that was a shift of energy, removing stuff. Sherry says, "If we are not at ease, we are in dis-ease, or disease." Still trying to save my life.

Henry called me to tell me he did not want to take the hedge fund internship that he was accepted to, he wanted to intern at a middle school outside Boston. Now that's a shift! He also told me he wanted to take the summer Yoga Teacher Training with Sherry. Another shift. That was great. Not only would it be a deep soul journey, I would be able to be with him all summer! Will did the training the year before, so good for broken hearts. Still, Grace left.

For me, the healing practices work. Moving energy around and out so we can sit in Sukhasana, easy seat. Clear mind, clear heart.

*Menemsha, Day of Healing Invitation*

*April 1, 2017*

*It is no worse than any other day. Same thing, wake up, think of you, imagine a scene of our lives. What if I did this on that day. Sip my coffee, look out the window, hold the warm cup to my face. Tears fall, stare. Today is no different. I thought it would be worse. Two years, ten years, it doesn't matter, they are years without you. Me without you. I'm on the Vineyard. I felt it would be a little better. It's not. It is pouring rain just like last year. This year only Henry is here, everyone else on their own. Trying to figure out life without you. What I could have done differently. It all does not matter, though.*

*I have continued to try to reach you. To sit quietly and try to see your face. You are not in my dreams as much as I would like, where are you? I want to be able to see you and know you are safe and that I will see you again. And if not, just darkness, nothingness? I don't know, I am going to spend the day editing our book. I got my tattoo of the fish, I like it. They remembered you at Ink Side Out, where you got your tattoos. You were trendy, that's for sure. Well, I am honoring you today on this crying day. Two years alone. I need my baby back. Come back, please.*

*Mom xo*

*My Family, Menemsha Harbor*

# COMPASSION

Following the events of April 1 through June of 2015, after Jack left us, Will, Henry, Grace and I retreated to Chowder Kettle Lane. The familiar bunk beds, Jack's empty. We needed to be together, but then there was Kevin, what do we do about this? Two months before, I was so angry with him. The divorce was so traumatic. What now? Days following Jack's death, just two weeks since the dissolution of our twenty-six year marriage, it ends up Kevin and I are in the house alone. Staring into space, circling around the kitchen. I was preparing dinner for the two of us. How could this be possible?

When we retreated to Martha's Vineyard, Kevin came. He needed his family. He loved Jack like we all did, and we were all so sad and needed each other.

My kids were confused at us being together when we had just ended it all. I was confused, too. They asked if we were getting together again.

"No," I said. "We are not. I think this is called compassion."

Nothing else mattered, it surpassed everything. I couldn't harbor any resentment and anger on top of the sadness and grief. I think this is what compassion looks like, providing space and support for those who are hurting, despite the wrongs and hurts of the past.

I told my kids that I have made a choice not to carry the burden of negative feelings, I feel that way still now. We all have a choice.

"You are the sum total of everything you've ever seen, heard, eaten, smelled, been told, forgot—it's all there."
— Maya Angelou

soul...

*Art Journal page, The Soul*

# HIGHER CONSCIOUSNESS

In my dreams, I could never hold Jack. Last night was different. We were in the kitchen at home. I was facing the interior of the kitchen. Jack came behind me and wrapped his arms around my neck, a giant Jack hug. I looked to the right and there he was, looking back right into my eyes, hazel eyes, just like mine, with a brown freckle. "You're back. Grace, it's Jack!" He reached his right arm ahead pointing and speaking to someone. I don't know who it was because I couldn't keep my eyes off him.

I woke startled as always, and closed my eyes so I could return to him. I slept and he was there in another way, it was vague and now I can't remember.

Grace and I have very vivid dreams, Emily too. I have found that they are called lucid dreams, a dream where the dreamer is actually aware they are dreaming and can exhibit some control. But there is more to it. A level of consciousness.

Deepak Chopra conducted a seminar that I watched on YouTube on the levels of consciousness. Summarizing the seminar from the ancient seers, there are seven layers of consciousness. The first is Deep Sleep. "In Deep Sleep there is some awareness, as when a mother is sleeping but can sense when her baby is fussy or needs to be fed, some awareness."

In the second level, there are more experiences than deep sleep. It is the Dream State. There are interactions with the environment, relationships. There are subject/object splits. I see myself as a person, subject, other people and things in the dream are the objects. There are tastes, smells, sound, all the senses. It is reality in that realm. That is where I meet Jack. It is not nearly as often as I would like. Before I go to sleep I call him in, to come meet me in my dream. It doesn't always work, but I have read that it helps. The third level is the Waking State. Awake, reality, interactions with other awake beings. This is the level that is conventionally perceived as "reality." So, the waking state is real? Well, yes, it's real for the waking state. When I am dreaming, it is real too, it is real in the dream state. Relative reality. So, it is true, it was real. All the dreams, me and Jack, it was real. I want to go to sleep right now!

Traditional wisdom calls the fourth level the Transcendental Consciousness, or a "glimpse of the soul." Where consciousness transcends, goes beyond. It transcends the world we live in of space, time, and causality (this causes this and that), the five senses. The soul is not of this world. The soul is an entity of "acausality, non-local quantum mechanical, interrelatedness," is what Deepak called it. "The soul is beyond space and time, has no cause, no location, instantly synchronized with everything else." "Water can not wet it, fire can't burn it, wind can't dry it, weapons can't destroy it, it is unborn, so never dies." This level of consciousness can be experienced through meditation. Rumi, the Suffi poet said, "This is not the real reality, real reality is behind the curtain, in truth we are not here, this is our shadow."

In the fourth level is where intuition develops, where one finds the hidden meaning behind events, where our dreams become meaningful. The inner and outer world connect. Senses are fine tuned, health improves, toxic habits fade, relationships improve when spending time in this meditative state. Quality of life improves. There are actual scientific studies of the brain activity in each of these states, the brain waves change in each level of consciousness.

The fifth level in the wisdom tradition is called Cosmic Consciousness or Christ Consciousness. In the Bible, it was written, "I am in this world but not of it." "Simultaneity of local and non-local awareness," says Deepak. Observing the body from the spirit form. The witness of all roles the body and mind play through a life time. "I am the alert witness of the roles I play, spirit is not the role I play," says Deepak. In the yoga science, this is called Lila, the Divine comedy. So many roles over so much life, this life and others. I can only recall me as a young child, teenager, student, nurse, girlfriend, wife, mother, executive, so many roles. I am the alert witness of the roles I play in my Divine comedy. In this level, there are "synchronistic, meaningful coincidences." Yes, I know this state, I call it evidence, and I log it down. In this state, there is a flow with the universe. Shawn would say that it's like getting in the river and floating, just flowing with the current.

Divine Consciousness or God Consciousness, is the sixth state. Witnessing awareness, fully awake. The universe is living consciousness, alive just like me. Nature becomes alive. Nature breathes out and we breathe in. The universe is always changing, everything becomes miraculous. "There is nowhere you can go where God is not. This level is transformation, healing, bliss."

Lastly, "The witness of subject and witness of object become one, Unity Consciousness." I love this. Deepak uses the analogy of a drop of water that is part of the ocean, "Why limit a drop to a drop when it is all of it. Not only the ocean, but the vapor, the clouds, the rain and river, waterfall and back to the ocean. Just like us, we are all of it, why limit, we are spirit in every form. Fetus, baby, teenager, adult, we are all one, unity. Unborn never dies."

*July 19, 2016*

*Dear Jack,*

*I dreamt of you last night. I could wrap my arms around you and bury my head in your chest. You were younger. The last time I had a dream with you I was able to wrap my arms around your stomach and I said, "Jack you're back!" It was so real. I woke in tears. I miss you. I would rather live in the dream, in that state of consciousness, it is my reality. Why not? Who is to say this waking state is reality? I want the other one more.*

*Art Journal page, Smoke*

# THE NATURE OF REALITY

Through the yoga practice and trying to heal myself, since I am the only one who can, I have explored my internal landscape through all the Koshas, or layers of the body. We focus so much on our one physical body, but in the science of yoga there are many more. The breath body, energy body, emotional body, intuitive body, bliss body. Also in the yoga science, the physical body is not just what we touch on our skin, but the food we eat, the company we keep, music we listen to, what we read. It makes sense. It all makes sense. But where I have been focusing more and more is on the intuitive body and the bliss or spirit body. In addition to the attention to the layers of myself, I heal my internal world through balancing the chakras or energy wheels in the body. You won't find them if cut open during a surgery. They are energy, vitality. Seven centers starting at the pelvic floor and continuing up through the crown of the head. With each chakra there is an associated color and a sound. The crown of the head, or seventh chakra, is pure white light, the sound is the vibration of the sound Om, silent. Here in the white light, at the crown of the head, bathed in the vibration of Om, is how we connect with spirit. We ourselves are the bridge between heaven and earth.

Balancing the chakras is a way to heal ourselves. Focusing on the different regions, breathing, and certain yoga poses can help to balance the chakras. Meditation is a way to focus on the seventh chakra. Most people I have spoken with about meditation find it difficult. I agree. I try to meditate daily. I have found it very helpful to use guided meditations. I like Deepak Chopra meditations because his voice is calm and soothing. He suggests a centering thought and a mantra to repeat when the mind begins to drift. A mantra is a word or phrase repeated, that is often used in meditation or even in prayer.

Prayer, that is a word I haven't used in a while. As I continue to discover or expand my higher mind or consciousness, my perception has changed on most every level. Prayer to me is now intention. God to me is now The Universe. The Bible to me is teachings and lessons that are universal, every religion has them. To me, they are individuals storytelling, and later documenting unexplainable events which are timeless. So many miracles, events that can not be explained. I call it evidence. I no longer believe there is one way to God. My God, My Universe is too expansive to have a one and only way. I believe I was misinformed. We all have access to the Divine. We can plug in to the Source of all things anytime. We are all spiritual beings clothed in flesh. The Divine is in us.

Leaving no stone unturned, I naturally have been using Oracle Cards. My favorite set are the Energy Oracle Cards, by Sandra Anne Taylor. I have a set from Lisa Williams, too, but I gravitate to the first. Using these cards is a way to develop intuition, that word again. We have the power to change and transform our lives, it's all energy, and the cards foster that shift.

It is no surprise that when leaning toward a chapter on higher consciousness, I pulled card #32 from the deck. First, I fanned the deck over my heart, I created my intention to deliver a clear and concise message for my day by drawing one card. I shuffled the deck and flipped the first card. In this deck, there is a reading from the guide book for a card presented upright and also reversed. I pulled an upright card, "Door to Spirit" #32, Spiritual Awakenings and New Beginnings.

"This door opens onto the expansive energetic realm where all new beginnings originate. The orbs of light are guiding you through the cloud of the earthly world, leading you to a deeper understanding of your eternal identity, the source of all true value and power. (I have learned the orbs of light are spirit energy. People post them all the time on Facebook and YouTube. I've looked for them in darkened rooms, but I haven't seen anything.) This door opens onto truly unlimited potential, for the changes that happen here reach deep into the core of your being. As such, this card often heralds your increasing connection with the spirit world. Don't be surprised if you find yourself becoming more intuitive, more aware of spirit's presence, or more powerful in your own healing practices. Now is the time to open up to the unexpected guidance and inspiration of spirit and to the magic and power of your true identity!"

*Art Journal page, Secrets Revealed*

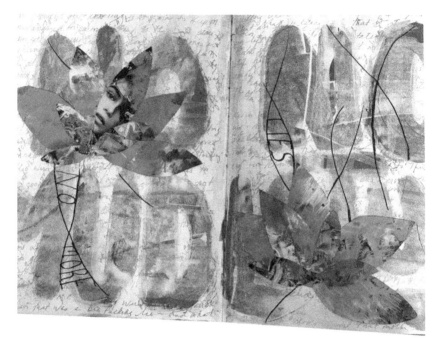

*Art Journal page, No Mud No Lotus*

# NO MUD, NO LOTUS

In the wisdom traditions, the lotus flower is a symbol of purity, rebirth, divinity and beauty. The different traditions have slight variations on the meaning of the eight-petal flower. The lotus's different colors represent different meanings as well, but all seem to agree that the flower appears clean and pure against the background of a dirty pond. The exquisite lotus flower blooms from dark, murky water.

In the Buddhist tradition, the bud appearing from the muddy waters symbolizes a person following a path of spirituality, leaving attachment behind. The bud blossoming symbolizes the person's true awakening. The Hindu tradition is rather complex and offers many perspectives, both on awakening and creation. The Deities are often portrayed with the lotus flower, representing those in the highest standing. One can also observe the lotus flower in Egyptian hieroglyphics. The flower retracts at night back into the dark waters and blossoms the next day, representing new birth.

The lotus has significant meaning in my life. I lived in the murky water, closed and dark, for a long time. The world around me was unclear, so many un truths, so much chaos, kept me closed for my own protection. How much of life I missed, it makes me sad. I completely lost my true self, my little girl Barbara self. Closed like the bud of the lotus, hidden in muddy waters.

I am awake now. Coming from the dark and into the light is no exaggeration, rebirth. With tremendous strife, I grew out of the mud and I believe I am now the beautiful flower I was designed to be. I am now my true self. And it was beyond difficult getting to this place. I continued to work with Shawn and do the assigned homework to keep myself moving forward. She said, and Jack said (she is a medium too, and is just starting to focus on this area of work), the inner child is our true essence. That little girl, my soul crying out for attention, to feel safe and not ignored.

Shawn had me remember a time when I was under ten, a memory that made me so happy. It came to me immediately. I must have been five or six and I was given a gift of a light blue dress. It came from my parents' friend in Scotland; her name was Barbara, too. It had lace and netting under the skirt which made the dress puff out. I never saw anything more beautiful in my life. I wanted to wear it so badly to a birthday party that was outside, probably just playing around. I would be totally overdressed, but my mom let me wear it. Thinking of that moment gave me such joy. JOY? What was that again? Through this journey, this murky, dirty, muddy journey of my life, I am starting to peek through and see light. Through my daily practice of yoga, my daily meditation, my continuous road of searching and seeking, a petal or two are piercing through the darkness.

My last workshop was with Lisa Williams, the "famous" medium who read for my family on September 2. (She has her own TV shows, *Life Amongst the Dead* and *Voice from the Other Side*.) This workshop was at the Omega Center in Rhinebeck, New York. It was supposed to be a weekend with four hundred "awakened" people. There were only forty in our group. We were all there to learn to communicate with spirit. Apparently, we are all capable, we all have the innate ability, we just need to "remove the interference." Get rid of the stuff that clouds our minds and doesn't serve us. I've heard that before. Well, I have been working on that for years, so maybe I can talk to Jack directly, not through anyone.

I was determined, and still am, to communicate with my son, my baby, the true essence of Jack, so sweet, kind and loving. My God, I miss him so much. The training was more of a course in listening to our intuition, to trust, I mean TRUST. To set an intention to communicate with spirit.

We were to sit quietly and communicate with our partner what came to us. Trust that it was a message from spirit and speak whatever the message was. Well, I hope my partner didn't take my message to heart. I told my partner I felt her relationship was in trouble. There needed to be a separation, not a divorce, just space to regroup and clear the space to make well informed decisions. I don't know where that came from. My own experiences? Lisa said say whatever comes to you.

My next partner, I literally saw a ball and hands pushing it. So, I told her the image that came to mind. I felt it was time to "get the ball rolling," to get things started. She told me that in fact, she was contemplating making a move from her home, but there were many repairs before putting the house on the market. She said I was right, she needed to get the ball rolling. The first partner cried when I told her she needed space in her relationship. She said I was right, she and her husband had many problems, and she thought it best that he stay with his parents so she could have some space.

This intuitive stuff, I don't know if I have it or I don't. I think I am going to keep it mostly for myself. If I'm wrong, it would not be great for the people I am reading for.

I feel tuned in to my inner self, to my intuition. I sense when dark situations are approaching and I can set clear boundaries for myself, for my safety. There certainly aren't as many as in my past, but when I feel energy shifting, or sense personalities that do not support me fully. I just step away. When my kids or Kevin speak to me in a way that feels threatening to me, I step away. It allows me to reacquaint myself with me, rebirth. I always liked myself. I tried my best, worked hard, thought I was respectful, kind, and a good friend. Then the darkness, the mud, the closed bud.

Following my internal compass, my own intuition, loving myself, attracts people to me supporting my journey and my awakening. My inner beauty is coming through. The lotus, clean and pure against the background of the dirty pond. That was the background now, it is in the past and I am not attached.

## GRIEF

*I had my own notion of grief.*
*I thought it was a sad time*
*That followed the death of someone you love.*
*And you had to push through it*
*To get to the other side,*
*But I'm learning there is no other side.*
*There is no pushing through.*
*But rather,*
*There is absorption*
*Adjustment*
*Acceptance*
*And grief is not something that you complete*
*But rather you endure*
*Grief is not a task to finish,*
*And move on,*
*But an element of yourself -*
*An alteration of your being.*
*A new way of seeing,*
*A new definition of self.*

# IT'S AN INSIDE JOB

"Take care of yourself." Do people really know what that means? For years, I have been told to take care of myself during strife and stressful times. I thought, if one more person tells me that, I am going to punch them in the nose. What does that mean, take care of yourself? I ate well, I practiced yoga, I took care of my personal and mental health. Is that not enough? But as the tragedies continued to mount, it was not enough. I could not maintain my health and wellness with external means. The only way out was in.

I learned that as I continued to work on myself, practice, practice, practice, in all areas, the external started to become less of an influence and the subtle internal began to shift. Healing comes from within. No one can do it for us. You can't talk through it, there is no way around it, only through it.

I received this poem from someone. There was no author attached.

You don't push through it, it becomes you. Yes, it's true. It is me, the new me. The me without Jack, is a new definition of self, an alteration of my being. I don't know who I would be without it. Grief becomes your friend. I remember this from Harry. It is a life-altering experience, staying close to this friend you think will keep you close to your love. But no. What gets you closer to your love is to clear the static, remove what is in the way, and then it begins, the real work. Soul work. It is an inside job. I am my own healer, teacher, goddess. So are you. So are we all. No one can do the work for us. We have all we need, we are magnificent creations prepared and designed to heal ourselves.

My yoga practice has helped me to clear out the stuff that doesn't serve me, leaving me with me and my grief. Going from practicing every day in a filled studio with music and crazy arm balances, twists and head stands, teaching eight classes a week, to retreating to my studio, listening to a guided meditation, practicing quietly for twenty minutes and sitting quietly trying to connect to spirit, ending with the endless flow of tears.

My practice has become a meditative one. I am trying to work on my mind clearing with mantra, guided meditation, and continuing my journaling.

The subtle body is fascinating. The more I practice physically, layering on meditation, the more the layers peel away. It's like adding on in reverse. Peeling away the self judgment, the external, and I am left with me and the everlasting longing to reach spirit, Jack.

Yearning, longing, it can't be described.

*Art Journal page, Happiness, an inside job*

*Art Journal page, What Love Is*

# LOVING WHAT IS

Loving what is? How do you do that? So much suffering, how do we love what is? When there is nothing we can do, we have to not only accept our situation, but love it? Accepting is hard enough, I can't even do that. The repeated self-talk, what if I did this or that, I did everything I could, I didn't do enough. Round and round and there is nothing I can do now. Jack is gone. Sometimes I can accept it, and other times the overwhelming loss covers me with darkness. Love what is? On my retreat to Omega to work with Lisa Williams, 200 other awakened people were there to see Byron Katie. The author and speaker packed a full house. I sat for lunch with a woman attending her seminar. She was thin and frail. Her head was bald and I assumed she was in cancer treatment, but we didn't talk about that. She was there to do "The Work," the system Katie developed to aid in this redirection of patterned behavior. She handed me a worksheet. Loving what is? So was my lunch mate trying to love and accept her situation? She was sweet, I bought the book.

Katie says, "Suffering is optional." That when we believe our thoughts, or "our story," we suffer. She asks the question, "But is it true?" She has designed a powerful system of self-inquiry that allows the practitioner to identify and "question the thoughts that cause so much suffering." The process, "The Work," uses a worksheet to help guide the process. She said, in her talk that when she didn't believe her thoughts she experienced joy, and that it had always been there. Hmmm.

*Art Journal page, Just One Star*

# WE ARE STAR DUST

In yoga class, I have been hearing over and again from Sherry that we are made of the same chemical make up as stars. "We are star dust." I looked it up: nitrogen, oxygen, carbon, a few other elements. I've listened to that for years. Never really gave it much thought though. "You hear it when you hear it." Well, in a Skype session with Shawn, she said it, and I heard it.

I have been stuck in the blame game for quite a while. My broken family, my dreams not fulfilled, Jack's development and all my kids, embarrassed and humiliated in my community, a ripple effect with all my friends and family, financial and emotional burdens. The story has been playing in my head for years. It is my story, yes, but is it true? Shawn said, "You know we are all star dust. Stars don't blame each other, they are just on a journey."

I finally heard it. This is part of my journey. Why I chose this, I am not quite sure, but it is my journey. Kevin has his. Jack has his. We are all stars on our journey, and stars don't blame each other.

*March 30, 2016*

*Jack,*

*You weren't there when I looked in my dreams. Something weird was going on. I did think I saw the letter J carved into something. Was that a sign?*

*I had my astrology chart read by Patricia, the Argentinian translator on the Shaman retreat in Beverly Hills. I loved her disposition. We had our session over Skype. So interesting. She said it was my nature to do my best. I believe that. I always do my best. I am blamed for so much. What I fed you guys, how I handled you, the divorce I'm sure. I know they love me, my family, but they still blame me. She said to me that the Sun is moving into Pisces. Pisces, she said, is the sign of opening up to the new, the unseen, and the loss of grief and chaos. The Sun in Pisces, that sounds about right. Settling into the spirit connection. She said clairvoyance could come during this time, cool. I'm open, I don't want to be afraid. God help me to open up to receive messages from spirit so I can join in the healing energy of this planet.*

*I need to sit with this information. Not hold on to the past, yet not grasp the first thing that comes along. I don't know anything about astrology, all of the stars and planets, but be certain I will find out.*

*She said when my heart has healed a little bit more she will read your chart for me. Maybe then I can understand more of you and why this happened. It's impossible to let go. I don't want to because I love and miss you. I guess I'll know when I know. Trying to surrender, let go. Trying. Thank you Jack.*

*Mom xo*

# JACK IN A BOX

This has been an incomprehensibly difficult journey. What I know to be true is that grief is not something you get over, it is something you have to endure. There are no words to describe the pain and suffering of losing your child or in my case children. There are no rules for grief, but what I know for sure is that grief becomes a friend. When grief subsides, it's as though we have to go back to normal life, whatever that is. It is comforting to be in the sad, dark and lonely place, it is too bright out in the world.

What I know to be true is that we should never ever stop helping the ones we love. We need to look outside the box for treatments and roads that lead to healing. The traditional shit doesn't work. Cut him out of your life, leave him on the street. No, that's not going to work, and that is all I was told. Get informed! It happens to those who least expect it.

We need to get the drugs off the streets and out of the hands of our children. Prescription drugs are over prescribed and groups like Shatterproof are working to change legislation to monitor distribution. Ibogaine treatment centers, hallucinogens like ayahuasca, and spiritual healings are alternatives, seek them out. Ibogaine is an ancient sacred root used in healing ceremonies. It is known to put people in a "dream state." The participant is guided through a conversation with "self," confronting fears that hold one back. It is said to be the most effective treatment for addiction, particularly opiods. Ayahuasca is a powerful hallucinogenic plant medicine that allows the participant to travel deep into the mind and subconscious.

Twelve Steps isn't the answer for kids holding smoking guns. That's maintenance. They don't have the time that it takes to spend years in AA, they die fast. I continue to research alternatives for others. It is too late for me and Jack, but there are options. There are addiction specialists that support the addict in finding the appropriate individualized care that they need. The rehabs have a template that works for some, but obviously was not the right formula for Jack. There are Harm Reduction Organizations that provide a safe environment for users, overdose protection and support versus attaching a stigma to those in need.

Drastic measures need to be taken for a drastic situation.

Addiction is a disease and the stakes are high. Opioid and heroin overdoses are increasing at alarming rates. These drugs are killing a generation of kids. They killed mine.

What I know to be true is that regret is just as bad a grief. Maybe worse. The hours and days all Jack's family regret not returning the call or text, going for a visit, having a heart to heart conversation about his life's direction.

Don't regret anything, do everything.

A catastrophic event like this and its explanations did not fit in my belief system, my awareness or consciousness. It did not fit in this box called my life. I had to expand and will continue through all the levels of my consciousness. "You can't put Jack in a box." The box of this life experience had him boxed in, he had to expand, and I'm right behind him. Think outside of the box.

*Art Journal page, Outside the Box*

**SO MANY PEOPLE**, I can't see their faces, it seems like a mass of bodies. Breathe, take it slow. This is worse then the front row. Standing in the ultimate front, facing everyone. I want to savor every word and swallow them as they become me. Me and you. I continued...

This my love is my final love letter, one I never wanted to write.

*Dear Jack,*

*I am desperate without you. I know you are at peace. Please watch over us as Dad, Will, Henry, Grace and I start down this road without you. I have much invested in this place we call Heaven, my dearest souls abide there. This is too much for us to bear, but we find comfort knowing you are safe.*

*I am so mad at you for leaving us. I know our souls will be together again and we will soar on eagles wings, together in true love.*

*Forever and ever my love,*

*Mom*

Dear Mom,

I dont even know what to say at this point because nothing I say really means anything especially with the way I continue to act here. Something I really struggle with is expressing my emotions because for so long i have trained myself to not feel anything so I could continue to lie, cheat and steal from you and many others. And the most frustrating part is that I am going to need to train myself to feel and care for the people i love. I have put you through hell with my actions not taking into consideration the amount of stress you already have from everything with dad and will and having henry and grace in high school and all of the responsibilities you have already worrying about me and if I will be alive next week shouldn't be one of them. You have tried everything kicking me out, sending me to treatment etc. but I cant seem to get it right. Having you come into group put things in prospective for me and made me realize what i have and what im choosing to throw away. It was so good to see you and I know you werent here for me but still I appreciate you going to the end of the world for me. I have treated you with so much disrespect and am ashamed of the things i have done to you

212

like pawning your engagement ring, watch etc. trading other possesions for pills and stripping you of everything. I want you to know how sorry and guilty I feel about these things now and am going to take every step to get myself healthy and hopefully rebuild my relationship with you and my family if your willing. I will do everything it takes to make it right and that starts here, now getting better and sober, otherwise the only relationship I will have is with drugs until it kills me, and despite my actions thats not what I want for myself. But what im more interested in is you! how are you doing? Are you going to any meetings or support groups? im sure you are but I want to make sure your getting the help you need, I really hope your finding time for yourself through all of this because you deserve it, you should be the one in FL in the sun. I just want you to know I love you so much and miss you and hope to have some sort of communication with you. Hope I get a letter from you soon

love Jack.

*Art Journal page, Angel Wings*

## A SUMMARY OF ADDICTION FROM THE SHATTERPROOF WEBSITE:

"The disease of addiction claims more than 135,000 lives annually, making it the third largest cause of death in the United States, after heart disease and cancer. More than twenty-two million Americans suffer from addiction. At least one hundred million Americans suffer directly or indirectly from the disease, nearly one in three Americans. Those who are suffering from the disease and the millions who love them find their lives shattered."

"Our children are the victims. Unlike any other major disease, there is a narrow window when addiction develops: it nearly always originates during adolescence. The pre-frontal lobe, the area of the brain where decision-making, judgment and self-control reside, is the last area of the brain to develop, usually in the early twenties. Drugs arrest the development of the pre-frontal lobe and target the brain's reward system, literally changing brain circuitry."

"Addiction is similar to other diseases, such as heart disease. Both disrupt the normal, healthy functioning of the underlying organ, have serious harmful consequence, and are preventable and treatable."

Classic signs of addiction from the National Institute on Drug Abuse:

- Poor behavioral control
- Constant craving for drugs
- Inability to recognize serious problems with behaviors and relationships
- Continued drug use despite negative consequences

"Relapse rates for drug-addicted patients are similar to other chronic diseases, such as diabetes, hypertension and asthma. When treatment plans are not followed or do not work the patient will relapse. Hypertension and asthma have relapse rates from 50 to 70% of patients suffering from the disease. Drug addiction has a relapse rate of 40 to 50% and therefore drug addiction should be treated like any other chronic illness."

Gary Mendell, the Chairman and CEO of Shatterproof, founded the organization following the loss of his son, Brian, to addiction. His goal: to spare other families the tragedy his family suffered. "Shatterproof is a national non-profit dedicated to reducing the devastation that addiction to prescription drugs, illicit drugs and alcohol causes to families."

Thank You

My family
My dream girls
My countless friends

My teacher, Jack xo

# RESOURCES FOR ADDICTION AND RECOVERY

Vistit https://dearjackloveletter.com, for the most updated list and more resourses.

## BOOKS:

*With Love and Light*, Jamie Butler

*Anatomy of the Spirit*, Carlolyn Myss

*Talking to the Dead in Suburbia*, Anna Raimondi

*The Afterlife of Jimmy Fingers*, Annie Kagan

*Your Soul's Plan*, Robert Schwartz

*Healing After Loss*, Martha Whitmore Hickman

*Safe Passage, Words to Help the Grieving*, Molly Fumia

*Writing from the Heart*, Nancy Aronie

*My Son and the Afterlife*, Elisa Medhus, MD

*Loving What Is*, Byron Katie

*Many Lives, Many Masters*, Dr. Brian Weiss

*Life Among the Dead*, Lisa Williams

*Conversations with Mary*, Anna Raimondi

## VIDEOS/YOUTUBE:

- *Channeling Erik*
- *How to Start a New Life* – Wayne Dyer
- *Lisa Williams Audience Readings* (Uncut) | Studio 10
- *Why Don't Those Who've Died Communicate With Us More?* — Swedenborg and Life

## WORKSHOPS/RETREATS:

- Anna Raimondi Retreats
    Mothers Who Have Lost Children
    Annaraimondiretreats.com
- Melissa D'Antoni, Creative Alchemy
    Firetreestudios.com
- Nancy Aronie, Author

Chilmark Creative Writing Workshop
Nancyaronie.com
- Sherry Sidoti
  Yoga Teachers Immersion
  Flyyogamv.com
- Foster and Kristos Perry
  Shaman and Wicca
  Goldenhummingbird.com
- Lisa Williams
  Intuitive mediumship retreat
  Lisawilliams.com

Websites:
- AfterlifeTV.com
- LisaWilliams.com
- ChannelingErik.com
- AnnaRaimondi.com
- Swedenborg.com
- JamieButler.com
- TheTappingSolution.com

CPSIA information can be obtained
at www.ICGtesting.com
Printed in the USA
BVHW02*0819120718
521372BV00012B/57/P